HOW TO RAISE
AND TRAIN
A BRITTANY SPANIEL

Ch. Patrice de Sharvogue, owned by Dr. Edgar W. Averill, was the winner of the first specialty show of the American Brittany Club, in 1943.

By Edwin E. Rosenblum

Published by T.F.H. Publications   T.F.H. Building, 245 Cornelison Avenue, Jersey City, N. J. 07302. Distributed in the British Empire by T.F.H. Publications (London) Ltd., 13 Nutley Lane, Reigate, Surrey, England. In Canada by Clarke, Irwin & Company Ltd., Clarwin House, 791 St. Clair Avenue West, Toronto 10, Ontario, Canada. Printed in the U.S.A. by the lithograph process by T.F.H. Lithograph Corp., Jersey City, N. J. 07302.

Distributed to the Book Trade in the U.S.A. by Crown Publishers, Inc., 419 Park Avenue South, New York, N. Y. 10016.

To my mother and father

Cover photo by Louise Van der Meid.

Monique of Juan Chico, owned by John Barrett.

Contents

1. History, Characteristics, and Standard

ORIGIN

The rocky coast of Brittany juts out like a thumb from the corner of northwestern France, partially separating the English Channel from the great Bay of Biscay. This hilly, rugged peninsula, settled around 500 A.D. by fugitives from Britain, and where Breton (a Celtic language related to the ancient languages of Ireland, Cornwall, Wales, and Scotland) is still spoken in certain parts, is the birthplace of the Epagneul Breton—the Brittany Spaniel.

The Brittany Spaniel comes from an ancient lineage, possibly directly from the "original" spaniel line of Spain. In Great Britain this ancient spaniel line was developed into the "Springer-Cocker" types and the famous setters: the English, the Gordon, and the Irish, to say nothing of the many local strains or breeds that are today extinct or little known, such as the Red-and-White Setter of Ireland.

Setters were originally spaniels that were developed and trained by bird netters to point game and then drop low to allow a hunter to cast his nets over the sitting birds; this is in contrast to the flush (or "spring") of the Springer Spaniel, whereby the birds are frightened into the air.

Field Ch. Ronile Avant Courier on point. This typical Brittany aptly demonstrates the style and "birdiness" of his breed in the field.

In France the spaniel line underwent a similar process, with many local varieties of "springer" spaniels and "setting" spaniels being created. Some of these spaniels would be considered setters by today's standards. The Epagneul de Picardie, or Picardy Spaniel, from northeastern France, was one of these. About the size of a Gordon Setter, it was either all black or black with tan trim, or, occasionally, brown and gray. Another setter-like spaniel was the Epagneul Francais, or French Spaniel, whose dull white coat was marked with patches of chestnut color. A third breed was the Epagneul Ecossais, or Scottish Spaniel, which was very similar, if not identical, to the French Spaniel, but with orange instead of chestnut patches marking its white coat.

In addition to the purely local development of spaniels in France, there was undoubtedly also communication between the Breton people and the Celtic-speaking people of Scotland, Cornwall (extreme southeastern England and closest to Brittany), Ireland, and Wales. The possible close relationship between the orange-and-white Welsh Springer Spaniel and the Brittany Spaniel has been described by more than one writer. Indeed, it has also been said that the term "*Ecossais*" in the name Epagneul Ecossais refers not to the people of Scotland but to the Irish invaders of Brittany of some 1,500 years ago, who were known as the "Scoti."

Great Britain also boasted a setter-like dog known as the Scottish Spaniel, which was white with red fleckings. This dog is believed to have been a close relative of the Irish Setter and the Red-and-White Setter. Whether or not the Scottish Spaniel of Great Britain and the Epagneul Ecossais of France were identical dogs . . . or even closely related . . . is not known.

The French Spaniel, portrayed here as it appeared in the 1900's, is one of the Brittany's ancestors.

The Braque de Bourbonnais was used in the combination of breeds that were responsible for the Brittany Spaniel. It is from the Braque that the Brittany gets his pointing ability.

The Brittany Spaniel, which is essentially a small setter, may have been derived from any of the French "spaniel-setters" mentioned above or from some unknown local variety of the Brittany peninsula.

Legend has it that in the mid-1800's an English sportsman arrived in Brittany to hunt woodcock. He brought with him a lemon-and-white dog, presumably an English Setter, to assist him in this sport. While in Brittany this dog was crossed with a white-and-mahogany female spaniel belonging to a local hunter. The female's breed is not definitely known, but it was presumedly one of the French "spaniel-setters."

The resultant litter contained two tailless puppies. One, which later proved to be a prepotent (dominant) stud, continually sired litters containing short-tailed or tailless puppies. This unnamed dog is credited as the progenitor of the modern Brittany Spaniel.

The first time a dog officially listed as an Epagneul Breton was entered in a dog show was in 1896; this was Pincon-Royal, owned by the Viscount of Cambourg.

Another Brittany was shown in 1902. In that same year, a Brittany was also entered in a French field trial. These field trials were quite different from the modern American field trial: dogs were kept on leashes and rarely worked more than 15 minutes at a time.

Though they were beginning to gain recognition on the show bench (the first show award to a Brittany went to a dog named Max de Callac, in 1904) and in the field, the development of the Brittany Spaniel was far from over.

There were several distinct lines of Brittanies undergoing modification. The de Callac line, containing a number of black-and-white dogs, was being bred to French Spaniels from the Morbihan and Cotes du Nord sections of Brittany. (The show winner Max de Callac was reportedly the grandson of a black-and-red "setter.")

Another line, containing white-and-liver dogs, was crossed with British setters and pointers, especially one referred to in old books as the "Scotch Setter." No one knows for sure whether this was the Gordon Setter, Scottish Spaniel, or some other local Scottish strain.

Arthur Enaud, a French sportsman, who strongly preferred the orange-and-white coat pattern, strove to fix his favorite coloration in his line of spaniels. To intensify both the orange-and-white coloration and the pointing ability, Enaud crossed his Brittanies with two houndlike pointers carrying the orange and white color: the Italian Bracco and the Braque de Bourbonnais from central France. Judicious crossbreeding and back-crossing allowed Enaud's spaniels to retain their own breed conformation while reinforcing the orange-and-white coloration and the pointing instinct. Consequently, the Enaud line became quite popular and won general, but not necessarily complete, acceptance as *the* Brittany Spaniel.

The first breed standard was established in 1907. This originally called for black-and-white dogs, but this color was later dropped in favor of orange and white because it was feared that the former coloration allowed crossbred dogs recognition as Brittany Spaniels.

In 1908, white and tan colors were still seen. In that year Mirza, a dog of this coloration, won first place in a Normandy field trial. This color pattern, however, gradually disappeared from the breed.

THE BRITTANY IN AMERICA

In 1912 Louis Thebaud brought the first Brittany Spaniel to the United States, but no permanent breeding stock was established. In the 1920's several more Brittanies reached American shores, but again no breeding stock was established.

In the early 1930's Thebaud imported another Brittany that, unfortunately, was soon stolen. In 1934 and 1935 Thebaud and Clara G. Perry imported more Brittanies. The Perry dogs were the first Brittanies to be shown at the Westminster Kennel Club show in New York City.

From this point in the mid-1930's, the popularity of the Brittany climbed steadily. The first American field trial devoted entirely to Brittany Spaniels was held in 1939, with an entry of 14 dogs.

Until 1942, the Brittany Spaniel Club of North America was the primary breed organization. It had been accepted as the Brittany Spaniel parent club (with power to establish the breed standard) by the American Kennel Club. In 1942, the American Brittany Club was formed and was recognized by the American Field. The two clubs, with many of the same people belonging

The modern Epagneul. This cousin of the Brittany is similar to the early French Spaniel, instrumental in the Brittany's beginning.

Ch. Ultramend Ace High, owned and bred by Frank W. McHugh. Sire: Ch. Ultramend Valgo Crocker; dam: Ch. Ultramend Susie. This dog is shown winning best of breed at the Northern California Brittany Club. Photo by Norman.

to and holding offices in both, were soon merged, retaining the name of the younger club.

CHARACTERISTICS

Today the Brittany Spaniel is third in popularity of all the sporting breeds and seventeenth in popularity among all of the 115 breeds recognized by the American Kennel Club. The total 1963 A.K.C. registration of Brittanies was 6,660 dogs. This figure does not include those dogs registered with the American Field in its Field Dog Stud Book or those Brittanies whose owners simply never get around to registering them.

The Brittany is third among the sporting breeds, following the Cocker Spaniel and the Labrador Retriever. The former is rarely used as a hunting dog today, and the latter serves an entirely different function in the field. The Brittany, according to the A.K.C. registrations, is America's most popular pointing breed.

What accounts for the Brittany Spaniel's popularity? It has many factors in its favor. At an average weight of 35 pounds and an average height of 19 inches at the withers (the highest point of the back just at the base of the neck) and with a relatively short coat requiring little grooming, the Brittany Spaniel makes an ideal dog for the apartment-dweller and people who like to have their dogs ride with them in their cars instead of in the trunk (may their tribe increase!).

For the sportsman who hunts on foot, which includes the vast majority of hunters, the Brittany is ideal. He covers a sufficiently wide range in country where game may be relatively scarce, but you do not need a jeep to keep up with him. Further, the Brittany is more than just a pointer . . . he is also an excellent retriever.

The Brittany is one of the few hunting breeds in which the majority of breeders are concerned with both hunting ability and body conformation. It is not uncommon for a Brittany field trial champion to be a bench champion as well.

The Brittany is a sensitive dog, so harsh or rough treatment or training techniques may more likely ruin him than help him. A firm tone of voice or even a harsh look is generally sufficient correction for a Brittany. Yet the Brittany is not a timid dog; he loves a rough and tumble romp with other dogs and with youngsters.

STANDARD

GENERAL DESCRIPTION—A compact, closely knit dog of medium size, a leggy spaniel having the appearance as well as the agility of a great ground coverer. Strong, vigorous, energetic and quick of movement. Not too light in bone, yet never heavy-boned and cumbersome. Ruggedness, without clumsiness, is a characteristic of the breed. So leggy is he that his height at the withers is the same as the length of his body. He has no tail, or at most, not more than four inches.

WEIGHT—Should weigh between 30 and 40 pounds.

HEIGHT—$17\frac{1}{2}$ to $20\frac{1}{2}$ inches—measured from the ground to the highest point of the back—withers.

Disqualification—Any Brittany Spaniel measuring under $17\frac{1}{2}$ inches or over $20\frac{1}{2}$ inches shall be disqualified from bench show competition. Any black in the coat or a nose so dark in color as to appear black shall disqualify. A tail substantially more than four inches in length shall disqualify.

COAT—Hair dense, flat or wavy, never curly. Not as fine as in other spaniel breeds, and never silky. Furnishings not profuse. The ears should carry little fringe. Neither the front nor hind legs should carry heavy featherings.

Note: Long, curly, or silky hair is a fault. Any tendency toward excessive feathering should be severely penalized, as undesirable in a sporting dog which must face burs and heavy cover.

SKIN—Fine and fairly loose. (A loose skin rolls with briars and sticks, thus diminishing punctures or tearing. But a skin so loose as to form pouches is undesirable.)

COLOR—Dark orange and white, or liver and white. Some ticking is desirable, but not so much as to produce belton patterns. Roan patterns or factors of orange or liver shade are permissible. The orange and liver are found in standard parti-color, or piebald patterns. Washed out or faded colors are not desirable. Black is a disqualification.

Ch. Starbelle Penny, owned and handled by Lee Sleeper and bred by Dorothy Morehouse. Sire: Dual Ch. Belloaks King; dam: Torchette of Lionheart. Penny is shown in a win under Dr. J. E. Redden at the Newton Kennel Club. Photo by Evelyn Shafer.

SKULL—Medium length (approximately $4\frac{3}{4}$ inches). Rounded, very slightly wedge-shaped, but evenly made. Width, not quite as wide as the length (about $4\frac{3}{8}$ inches) and never so broad as to appear coarse, or so narrow as to appear racy. Well defined, but gently sloping stop effect. Median line rather indistinct. The occipital crest only apparent to the touch. Lateral walls well rounded. The Brittany should never be "apple-headed" and he should never have an indented stop. (All measurements of skull are for a $19\frac{1}{2}$ inch dog.)

MUZZLE—Medium length, about two thirds the length of the skull, measuring the muzzle from the tip to the stop, and the skull from the occipital crest to the stop between the eyes. Muzzle should taper gradually in both horizontal and vertical dimensions as it approaches the nostrils. Neither a Roman nose nor a concave curve (dish-face) is desirable. Never broad, heavy, or snipy.

NOSE—Nostrils well open to permit deep breathing of air and adequate scenting while at top speed. Tight nostrils should be penalized. Never shiny. Color, fawn, tan, light shades of brown or deep pink. A black nose is a disqualification. A two-tone or butterfly nose should be severely penalized.

EYES—Well set in head. Well protected from briars by a heavy, expressive eyebrow. A prominent, full, or pop eye should be heavily penalized. It is a serious fault in a hunting dog that must face briars. Skull well chiseled under the eyes, so that the lower lid is not pulled back to form a pocket or haw for catching seeds, dirt, and weed dust. Judges should check by forcing head down to see if lid falls away from the eye. Preference should be for darker-colored eyes, though lighter shades of amber should not be penalized. Light and mean-looking eyes to be heavily penalized.

EARS—Set high, above the level of the eyes. Short and leafy, rather than pendulous, reaching about half the length of the muzzle. Should lie flat and close to the head, with the tip rounded very slightly. Ears well covered with dense but relatively short hair, and with little fringe.

LIPS—Tight to the muzzle, with the upper lip overlapping the lower jaw only sufficiently to cover under lip. Lips dry so that feathers do not stick. Drooling to receive a heavy penalty. Flews to be penalized.

TEETH—Well-joined incisors. Posterior edge of upper incisors in contact with anterior edge of lower incisors, thus giving a true scissors bite. Overshot or undershot jaw to be penalized heavily.

NECK—Medium length. Not quite permitting the dog to place his nose on the ground without bending his legs. Free from throatiness, though not a serious fault unless accompanied by dewlaps. Strong, without giving the impression of being overmuscled. Well set into sloping shoulders. Never concave or ewe-necked.

BODY LENGTH—Approximately the same as the height when measured at the withers. Body length is measured from the point of the forechest to the rear of the haunches. A long body should be heavily penalized.

WITHERS—Shoulder blades should not protrude much. Not too widely set apart with perhaps two thumbs' width or less between the blades. At the withers, the Brittany is slightly higher than at the rump.

SHOULDERS—Sloping and muscular. Blade and upper arm should form nearly a 90-degree angle when measured from the posterior point of the blade at the withers to the junction of the blade and upper arm, and thence to the point of the elbow nearest the ribs. Straight shoulders do not permit sufficient reach.

BACK—Short and straight. Slight slope from highest point of withers to the root of the tail. Never hollow, saddle, sway, or roach-backed. Slight drop from hips to root of tail. Distance from last rib to upper thigh short, about three to four fingers in width.

CHEST—Deep, reaching the level of the elbow. Neither so wide nor so rounded as to disturb the placement of the shoulder bones and elbows, which causes a paddling movement, and often causes soreness from elbow striking ribs. Ribs well sprung, but adequate heart room provided by depth as well as width. Narrow or slab-sided chests are a fault.

FLANKS—Rounded. Fairly full. Not extremely tucked up, nor yet flabby and falling. Loins short and strong. Narrow and weak loins are a fault. In motion the loin should not sway sideways, giving a zigzag motion to the back, wasting energy.

HINDQUARTERS—Broad, strong and muscular, with powerful thighs and well-bent stifles, giving a hip set well into the loin and the marked angulation necessary for a powerful drive when in motion. Fat and falling hindquarters are a fault.

TAIL—Naturally tailless, or not over four inches long. Natural or docked. Set on high, actually an extension of the spine at about the same level.

FRONT LEGS—Viewed from the front, perpendicular, but not set too wide as in the case of a dog loaded in shoulder. Elbows and feet turning neither in nor out. Viewed from the side, practically perpendicular to the pastern. Pastern slightly bent to give cushion to stride. Not so straight as in terriers. Falling pasterns, however, are a serious fault. Leg bones clean, graceful, but not too fine. An extremely heavy bone is as much a fault as spindly legs. One must look for substance and suppleness. Height to the elbows should approximately equal distance from elbow to withers.

HIND LEGS—Stifles well bent. (The stifle generally is the term used for knee joint.) If the angle made by the upper and lower leg bones is too straight, the dog quite generally lacks drive, since his hind legs cannot drive as far forward at each stride as is desirable. However, the stifle should not be bent as to throw the hock joint far out behind the dog. Since factors not easily seen by the eye may give the dog his proper drive, a Brittany should not be condemned for straight stifle until the judge has checked the dog in motion from the side. When at a trot, the Brittany's hind foot should step into or beyond the print left by the front foot. The stifle joint should not turn out making a cowhock. (The cowhock moves the foot out to the side, thus driving out of line, and losing reach at each stride.) Thighs well feathered, but not profusely, halfway to the hock. Hocks, that is, the back pasterns, should be moderately short, pointing neither in nor out; perpendicular when viewed from the sides. They should be firm when shaken by the judge.

FEET—Should be strong, proportionately smaller than other spaniels, with close-fitting, well-arched toes and thick pads. The Brittany is not "up on his toes." Toes not heavily feathered. Flat feet, splayed feet, paper feet, etc., are to be heavily penalized. An ideal foot is half way between the hare- and catfoot.

2. Breed Requirements

EXERCISE

Exercise is a controversial subject in the care and raising of dogs. Most authorities recommend exercise as a necessity for a dog, for apparently dogs, even more than human beings, tend to put on unhealthy fat if not exercised sufficiently. This is especially important in those dogs whose owners cannot help slipping them little tidbits from time to time.

Exercise, however, is *not* necessary for the health of your dog. Your dog can live a long, healthy life, if properly fed, with no more exercise than his daily walks—just as a sedentary office worker can be as healthy or healthier than a hard-working farmer or lumberjack. But like the office worker who drops dead while shoveling snow, do not expect your dog, merely because he is a dog, to run a mile or two, romp for an hour or so, or do any task of physical exertion if you do not keep him in good physical shape. To keep your dog in

Ch. Bonnie Kays Ricki's Image, owned by Bonnie Kay Holemo and bred by D. J. Frisch. Sire: Happy Hunter's Buster Brown; dam: Joy de Lune. This dog is shown winning the sporting group under judge Jerome N. Halle at the Macomb County Kennel Club. Photo by Norton of Kent.

good physical shape and in that smart, trim look a dog should have, he must be exercised. If you plan to hunt your dog, exercise is a must! It is not only unfair to take a soft dog out and expect him to turn in a hard day's work in the field—it is cruel! Do not think that just because your dog belongs to a hunting breed that he can sit around all year and be automatically prepared for the hunting season.

A good way to exercise your dog is to have two Brittany Spaniels and let them romp together for an hour or so every day, the longer the better. If you do not have two dogs, you can try "tailgating": have someone sit on the tailgate of a station wagon and hold your dog on a sufficiently long lead. Maintain just enough speed to keep the dog at a slow trot. Build up the length of your exercise periods slowly, perhaps only 15 minutes per period for the first week or so, and later to a half hour. Judge your speed and the duration of the exercise periods by your dog's ability to handle the exercise. You may also exercise your dog by having him run alongside a bicycle. Be particularly careful about traffic in these road exercises. Bicycling is also good for you, and if you are a hunter it will prepare you as well as your dog for the hunting season. Another form of exercise is to have your Brittany chase a ball that you throw for him.

DIET

For food requirements, a good high-quality dog food is best. Table scraps, while all right for an occasional treat or variety, should never form the bulk of your dog's diet. A diet based on table scraps is probably too rich and starchy and will surely lack the balanced nutrition necessary to keep a dog healthy. Do not buy low-quality dog foods; these are just packed with cereal grains and lack sufficient protein. Your dog may get plenty of bulk from these low-grade foods, but he will not receive the nutrition that his body needs. Both kibble (or meal) and canned foods are fine. During the hunting season your dog will probably need more fat to compensate for his increased output of energy than these foods provide. Additional fat may be supplied by bacon drippings or by a few small pieces of beef suet (the hard white fat from around the kidneys) placed on top of his food. Most dogs love both of these fatty foods.

COLLARS AND LEADS

The harness as part of a dog's gear belongs only on the sled dogs of the North or the cart-pulling dogs of Europe. For your Brittany a collar is the only proper neckwear. A light rolled-leather collar is best; a broad, flat collar will tend to flatten and wear down the hair on the neck. The standard length leash, or lead, three feet long, is quite satisfactory for walking. (For training gear see Chapter Five. If you fear a metal-link choke collar will catch in your Brittany's coat, a rolled-leather choke collar may be substituted.)

HOUSING

The Brittany Spaniel makes an ideal housedog and needs no outdoor kennel. If you do wish to keep your dog outdoors, however, make sure the doghouse does not rest directly on the ground, or dampness will make it a most unhealthy place for your dog. Set the doghouse on short, stout legs or on bricks at each corner. The doghouse itself should be at least 1½ times as high as the dog, and the sleeping quarters inside should be about twice as wide as the dog's height, or more. The roof should be slightly slanted to permit rain run-off; it should also be removable to facilitate cleaning. A roofed-over porch, as wide as the doghouse and from 1½ to 2 feet deep, provides an outdoor shelter for your dog and makes the doghouse much more serviceable. A doghouse with a draft-free sleeping quarters is especially good. This can be readily achieved by placing a partial wall inside the doghouse perpendicular to the door that will divide the doghouse into an entrance hallway and sleeping quarters. The dog enters the doghouse and proceeds along the short inside wall to the rear of the doghouse, turns around the far end of the wall, and then enters his sleeping quarters. A commercial dog door or a piece of heavy carpeting tacked across the door will help reduce the chill in winter. A floor covering of cedar shavings or similar bedding material is particularly important during the winter months. Adding insulation to the doghouse is always a good idea, for it minimizes both heat and cold. The doghouse should be well shaded in the summer or it will heat up like an oven.

If you keep your dog in a fenced run, the best run surface is probably concrete covered with a coating of plastic sealer. Such a surface is easiest to keep clean and yet does not permit parasites or their eggs to escape detection in the irregularities of an uncoated concrete surface. The fear that the non-resilient concrete will cause your dog's feet to become splayed is largely unfounded; at any rate, an occasional outing away from the concrete will suffice in overcoming any possible dangers.

GEOGRAPHIC LIMITATIONS

There are no geographic limitations for the Brittany Spaniel. Anywhere modern man can live, so can a Brittany. It is no secret, however, that the Brittany, like most dogs, prefers a cool, dry climate to one that is hot and humid.

GROOMING

Grooming the Brittany Spaniel is simplicity itself. Neither elaborate clipping nor special trims are required. Brush his coat daily with a good bristle brush; employ a comb for those areas where the brush does not provide maximum efficiency. Use a small narrow-bladed blunt scissors to trim the few odd hairs sticking out around his muzzle, and your grooming is finished.

Bathe your Brittany whenever he looks very dirty, but not too often, as this tends to dry out his coat.

3. Field Training

If you are one of the many people who do not care for hunting but are attracted to the Brittany Spaniel because of his many fine features, the Brittany is such an ideal dog that you can get the full enjoyment of his companionship without ever taking him hunting.

For the hunter, the active camaraderie and teamwork between you and your Brittany is an extra bonus few other breeds can offer.

If you plan to hunt with your Brittany, it is best that he come from hunting parents. This will at least mean that you are starting with a puppy that has a better likelihood of possessing the necessary degree of hunting and pointing "instinct" to increase your chances of success.

A very good idea is to write to both the American Field, 222 West Adams Street, Chicago, Illinois, and the American Kennel Club, 51 Madison Avenue, New York, New York, for a schedule of forthcoming Brittany field trials. Attend those nearest you and observe the techniques of the handlers and the performances of the dogs. This will give you, better than any book can, clear illustrations of what you should aim for with your dog. If any of the field trial techniques differ from those described here, use whichever you prefer.

No formal hunting training should be begun until the puppy is at least six months old; eight to ten months of age is much better, and decidedly preferable. At any age, however, take your puppy out into the field and let him romp, play, and flush and chase game as he pleases.

The hunting dog should fully understand and obey the basic, or yard, training commands of "No," "Sit," "Come," "Stay," and "Heel" (see Chapter Five) before embarking upon serious field training. Training should be conducted by one and the same person throughout; having too many trainers only confuses the dog and makes training much more difficult, if not impossible.

Training must be conducted every day, or you can forget about ever accomplishing anything. You cannot teach a dog only when the mood moves you and expect to get results. Early training lessons should be quite short, about five minutes or so, and held only once a day. Later the lessons can be increased to 15 or 20 minutes, twice a day. At this stage do not be afraid to teach more than one command at a time. If you wait until each command is thoroughly learned before proceeding to the next, training will take forever. You can use one lesson for one type of instruction and the second lesson for another type. Once command words and hand and whistle signals have been decided upon, never vary them. Never end training lessons abruptly or with punishment.

EQUIPMENT

Field-training equipment consists of a metal or leather choke collar (see Chapter Five); a sash cord, or similar line, about 25 feet or more in length; a hard rubber, bone, or Bakelite whistle (metal whistles will freeze to your lips if you hunt in cold climates); a stout lanyard, or whistle neck-cord, of plastic, chain, etc., for keeping the whistle handy around your neck and reducing the chance of its loss; a training pistol for firing .22 blanks (if you live in the city, a cap pistol will also be needed in the initial stages); and several training dummies, preferably the canvas-covered ones available at sporting goods stores, but reasonable facsimiles (such as a rolled and tied gunny sack of a size easy for the dog to grasp) will do. Many people use a length of broomstick or other hard object for training dummies, but as this may cause the dog to bear down with its teeth and tend towards a hard mouth, it is best to stay from such objects.

THE "WHOA" COMMAND

"*Whoa*," or "*Stop*," is a very important command for a bird dog; it is also basic to other phases of training. The teaching of this command can be done almost incidentally to the day's normal routine, at feeding time and during walks.

Place the choke collar and lead on your Brittany before feeding him. Have someone set the food dish some 15 feet away. When the dog starts towards his food, give the command "*Whoa !*", stop him, and hold him in place with the lead. Keep the dog at your left side, stroke him gently, and repeat the command "*Whoa*" again and again in a soft, soothing voice. After he has calmed down for a few moments, release him and allow him to proceed to his food on the command "*Hie on !*" given in an excited voice. ("*Hie*," which is an old word used by bird dog men, means to "go quickly.") You may accompany the command of "*Hie on*" with an underhand sweep of your left arm to familiarize your dog with this hand signal as well. Your excitement will generally be enough to convey to the dog that he no longer need remain in place; if it is not, a few running steps in the direction of the food, accompanied by another underhand sweep of your left arm and a repeat of "*Hie on !*", will be all the added inducement he will need.

Repeat this at every meal. When your Brittany obeys these commands well, increase the distance to his food and stop him two or three times in his approach to the food. Do not dispense with the lead until you are certain of his obedience.

This training can be supplemented during walks. As you walk your dog on a lead, give the command *"Whoa!"* and hold him in place (pet him and repeat the command as described above). Then command *"Hie on!"* and continue walking. Repeat this a number of times, but not for more than 15 minutes a day.

When obedience to *"Whoa"* is achieved, you should begin walking away from and around the dog as he holds in place to see if he will remain steady. Correct him as soon as he starts to turn or break. The final step is dispensing with the lead, giving the command *"Whoa,"* and having him hold steady in place as you walk away.

Once the hand signal for *"Hie on"* (described above) is learned, you may substitute the whistle signal (see "Quartering," in the section headed "Whistle Signals") for the vocal command.

FLASH POINTING

The trait of pointing game has been bred into your Brittany for generations. As an amateur trainer your task should be only to develop this trait, not teach it. Most Brittany Spaniel puppies, like the puppies of other pointing breeds, will "flash point" game without any training whatever. That is, when they come upon a game bird or game bird scent they will pause momentarily to hold that scent. This "flash point" is the nucleus that you will build on to develop staunchness, or steadiness, and style.

BRINGING ABOUT THE FLASH POINT

If you have an open field near you where birds abound, you are extremely lucky. Take your Brittany Spaniel out and let him romp and flush and chase birds: larks, sparrows—anything! Let him learn the fun and excitement associated with birds in the field. At various times your puppy will pause (flash point) before rushing in to flush the game. Regardless if the point is for a sparrow, pheasant, or chicken—encourage it. Repeat the *"Whoa"* command in a soft, reassuring voice. If he has learned this command well and holds in place, you are on the way to having a steady dog.

If the *"Whoa"* command is not yet learned, every time the dog holds the flash point long enough for you to reach him without dashing at him and causing him to break his point (try to approach him from the side rather than from behind, even pausing in your approach if you have to, to avoid startling him), kneel beside him and place one hand gently on his chest. With your other hand softly stroke him from head to tail, repeating, as you do, *"Whoa, Whoa"* in a soothing voice.

Try to keep him steady for no more than a minute or so, then step in and flush the birds with him, allowing him to chase them. Do not spoil his fun at this early stage by attempting to keep him steady to wing.

Continue this training until he remains staunch on point for several minutes. This achievement may take a few months. To intensify his staunchness, when your hand reaches his hindquarters as you stroke him and utter

The Brittany Spaniel is the only member of the Spaniel family that hunts by pointing. It is also one of the few sporting breeds where the bench and field dogs are of the same type.

the "*Whoa*" commands, gently press him forward very slightly; he will stiffen to resist this pressure and consequently improve his staunchness.

If your puppy is flash pointing but not holding for the "*Whoa*" command and you cannot seem to get up to him in time to steady him by hand, you will have to resort to the check cord method. Attach a sash cord to his collar. The recommended length is 25 feet, but it can be 25 yards if necessary and if he will drag that much line around. In any event it is a good idea to let the dog drag the sash cord around to grow accustomed to it before beginning his lessons. When he makes the momentary point, use the check cord to hold him in place until you can reach him. Apply a gentle, gradual pressure on the check cord; do not jerk it or pull the dog off his feet.

If you have no bird-filled field readily available or if your dog does not flash point, you will have to employ the rod and lure technique. This involves the use of a long stick or fishing rod, a line four to ten feet long, and a lure—a pheasant, quail, or other game bird wing is probably best, but lacking this any bird wing will do, or even an old rag or some crumpled paper. Rig the rod, line, and lure like a fishing outfit. Place the lure on the ground in front of the puppy, jiggling it to tease and attract him. Then, just as he tries to pick up the lure, pull it just out of his reach. When he realizes that every time he approaches the lure it moves away, he will pause and stiffen in front of it— the flash point! If you can reach him as he flash points, follow the procedure described above; if not, you will need an assistant to work the rod and lure for you. Do not use the rod and lure technique for more than a few weeks or you may train your dog to point moving objects, an undesirable trait known as false pointing.

As your Brittany grows steady on point, continually correct and staunch up any poor point. If he sets too low, prop him up into a more stylish form, praising and petting him as you do.

INTRODUCTION TO THE GUN AND GUN-SHYNESS

Although shyness and timidity can be inherited traits, it is safe to assume that virtually every gun-shy dog is, unfortunately, man-made. Careful introduction to the sudden, sharp, loud, and disturbing report of a gun is a critical point in the training of any hunting dog and should not be taken lightly.

Probably the best way to introduce a dog to the sound of gunfire is to shoot a .22 rifle or blank pistol when the dog is on one of his field romps and actually in the process of chasing a flushed animal: sparrow, rabbit, or what-have-you. Make sure the dog is at least 100 feet away—several hundred feet would be even better—when you fire. Do not fire more than once or twice during the first few introductory exercises. As the lessons proceed, gradually fire the .22 nearer and nearer to the dog. When he seems to accept the sound of the .22 without any fear, switch to a .410 shotgun, once more beginning at a distant range of 100 feet or more away from the dog. When the dog shows no concern for the .410, move up to the heavier gauges.

If your exercise field is somewhat shy of chaseable animals, you can wait until the dog has been taught to retrieve before introducing him to the gun. In this method, when you toss the dummy for a retrieve, have an assistant situated about 100 feet or more behind the dog fire the .22 when the dummy reaches the peak of its toss.

City dwellers who lack readily accessible fields may have to begin the introduction to the gun with the yard feeding and cap pistol technique. (A .22 blank pistol may be used initially instead of the cap pistol, or it may be substituted early in the training; the latter is preferable.) As one ill-timed shot may be disturbing enough to a puppy to start him down the road of gun-shyness, fire the cap pistol—once!—a good distance away from him while he is eating—not before. Repeat this at each feeding until the puppy completely ignores the shot. Gradually move in closer and closer to the puppy before firing. Later switch to the .22 blank pistol, once more beginning at the far distance. As the dog becomes accustomed to the firing of the gun it is a good idea to both increase the number of shots to two or three and to move the time of firing up closer and closer to the beginning of the meal. Eventually you will be firing when the dog is just beginning to eat and finally *before* he starts to eat. The shot will then become a signal calling the dog to eat—a pleasant association of the gun and shot for the dog.

RETRIEVING

Some trainers and dog experts do not believe that pointing breeds should be taught to retrieve. They consider as ideal the situation in which a hunter can use both a pointing dog to locate game and a non-slip retriever (Labrador,

Golden, etc.) to pick up the downed game. There is little doubt that such a combination is an excellent one and permits a more stylish action on the part of each dog. The average hunter, however, is simply unable to keep two dogs. This is particularly so in the case of Brittany people, who find this breed's relatively small size one of its most attractive features. Retrieving, therefore, is an important asset for your dog.

Retrieving can be taught by either of two basic methods: natural or forced. Natural retrieving training capitalizes on the retrieving "instinct" of the dog, rewarding him when he performs correctly. The dog, however, generally never considers such retrieving as anything more than just a game. If at times he does not feel like retrieving, he simply will not. Some trainers feel that natural retrieving is best, for with this system there is little danger of over-training a dog and making him rebellious. Such trainers are willing to risk the occasional display of non-cooperation.

Because the forced method is preferred in this book, the natural system will be only briefly described. Natural retrieving consists basically of arousing the dog's interest in the dummy (ball, sock, rolled gunny sack, etc.) before throwing it. Once he shows intense interest the dummy is thrown and the command "*Fetch!*" is given. The dog then dashes after the dummy and picks it up; as he does so you run back and away from the dog calling his name and clapping your hands so that he will chase after you with the dummy in his mouth. When he catches up to you, reach down and take the dummy from him. Do not let him drop it. Then pet and praise him. This is repeated one or two more times to complete the first lesson. As the dog progresses, the lessons increase in duration.

Forced training is used by the majority of trainers and is undoubtedly a more advantageous system from the viewpoint of the hunter. But if you have doubts or fears regarding the forced method, it would be best either to use the natural method or to send your dog to a professional trainer.

"FETCH!"

Begin this training where there is no possibility of distraction for the dog or interference with his training. Have your dog sit at your left side; grip his collar with the last three fingers of your left hand, leaving the thumb and forefinger free. Take the dummy and hold it in front of the dog's mouth. Keep his head down and to the front by a twisting pressure on the collar, if necessary. Push the dummy into the dog's teeth and command "*Fetch!*" If the dog does not open his mouth, squeeze his right ear between the thumb and forefinger of your left hand—do not pinch or dig your fingernails into his ear—and repeat "*Fetch!*" As soon as he opens his mouth to protest, push the dummy in and immediately release the pressure on his ear.

If he attempts to spit out the dummy, command "*Hold!*" and tap him under the chin with your right hand. When he does hold the dummy, pet and praise him. To make him release the dummy, grip the dummy firmly and say *"Give!"* (Do not pull the dummy while gripping or you will be teaching him to play tug-of-war with downed game.) If he does not obey, squeeze his ear again, commanding *"Give!"* as you do. Repeat this *"Fetch, Hold, and Give"* exercise only two or three times for the first few lessons, and give only one or two lessons a day. Remember, training must be conducted every day or you will get nowhere. A further word of caution: once the dog shows signs of tiring or losing interest in the lesson, do not force him to continue. Lessons should not be more than approximately 15 minutes long.

Once the *"Fetch, Hold, and Give"* training is thoroughly learned and the dog is picking up the dummy without collar or ear pressure, gradually, lesson by lesson, lower your hand holding the dummy until the dog is picking up the dummy from your hand as it rests on the ground. The next step, which surprisingly is a rather big one for the dog, is taking the dummy directly from the ground with your hand resting close by. Pet and praise him whenever he retrieves the dummy. Little by little and lesson by lesson move your hand farther and farther from where the dummy is resting on the ground.

If the dog refuses to pick the dummy up from the ground, go back to an earlier stage of the training where you were holding the dummy in your hand, and once more repeat the hand-lowering process. If, after a few lessons, he still refuses to pick the dummy up from the ground, resort to the collar and ear pressure technique to make him lower his head and open his mouth.

Once the ground pickup is learned, place the dummy a few feet in front of your dog before giving him the command to fetch. When he picks up the dummy, immediately call him back to you and take the dummy from him with the command *"Give!"*

If your dog balks at this stage, it is best to go back and repeat some of the earlier steps for a few lessons. If he still refuses, heel him out to the dummy, make him fetch, and then heel him back to his original position.

Gradually increase the distance of the retrieve; at first, however, it should be no more than 10 or 15 feet away.

A number of trainers use the dog's name instead of the word *"Fetch"* to command the dog to retrieve, primarily because this avoids confusion in field trials. The command-word *"Fetch"* is then used to mean *"Hold."* If you prefer this, use it.

If you plan to teach your Brittany to remain steady to wing and shot, hold him by the collar for a few seconds before releasing him to fetch. If this causes him to hesitate and become confused, dispense with it for a while.

On the long-distance retrieves, you can encourage your dog to return by calling his name, whistling, clapping your hands, and running back and away from the dog as he approaches. When he reaches you, quickly take the dummy from him with the command *"Give!"* Do not let him drop it, and do not pull the dummy from him.

STEADY TO WING AND SHOT

The dog that remains on point when the birds are flushed (steady to wing) and when the hunter fires (steady to shot) presents a polished, impressive performance; such performance is desirable in field trials. In actual hunting, however, its value is debatable. Many times a fast-breaking dog, which is practically under a falling bird, is a great asset even though his performance lacks "style." The decision is up to you.

There are two methods of steadying: one without employing a check cord, which is preferred because misuse of the check cord can lead to blinking (the habit of not holding a point or refusing to point at all), and one with a check cord.

For the first method, when you fire the gun, command "*Whoa!*"; if the dog has learned this command well, he will remain in place. Repeat this several times for several lessons to see if the dog is consistent in his obedience.

If your dog does not hold at the command of "*Whoa!*", go out to where he is and heel him back to the spot where he made his point. Keep him there for several minutes. Repeat this each time he breaks until he obeys the "*Whoa*" command at the shot.

The check cord system utilizes a line 25 to 50 feet long attached to the dog's collar. At the shot, command "*Whoa!*" If he breaks, let him go. Grasp your end of the check cord securely, and just as he reaches the end of the line command "*Whoa!*" once more and brace yourself. The sudden jerk when the dog reaches the end of the line will often throw him off his feet and even turn him head over heels. This technique usually takes only a few lessons.

WHISTLE SIGNALS

It is best to direct your dog in the field as little as possible. Let him make his own decisions. Overhandling can ruin a potentially good dog. Whistle signals are rather arbitrary: many trainers and hunters use the same signals to mean different things. With the preferable combination of hand and whistle signals, you need only two whistle signals: a short, sharp blast which means "*Sit!*" and a series of short blasts to call your dog in. The "*Sit*" whistle command will eventually come to mean to your dog that he is simply to pause wherever he is and look to you for further instructions rather than actually "sit."

Many trainers use two short, sharp blasts to make the dog turn and move in the opposite direction (quartering); other trainers use the same signal to mean "go straight out!" Some trainers use one long blast to call their dogs in. The selection is up to you. If you wish to use whistle signals for all important movements, it may be best to use the short, sharp blast for "*Sit!*"; the series of short blasts for "*Come!*"; two short, sharp blasts for going straight out ("*Hieing on*"); and one long and two quick shorts for quartering.

TEACHING TO QUARTER

There are several methods of teaching to quarter: one involves the dog's learning to follow your own quartering walk, with or without whistle signals; another involves the dog's following hand signals on the retrieve; and still another employs the check cord.

For the first method, select a distant point straight ahead of you as your goal. Send the dog out with the familiar underhand swing of your left hand and arm. Start walking forward and to your right until you are about 15 yards to the right of the midline. At this point turn and walk forward and to your left until you are about 15 yards *left* of the midline. Your dog should follow your zigzagging walk. As the lessons progress, cut down the amount of your zigzagging; the dog should continue his.

The addition of whistle signals usually helps the dog to understand what you would like of him. When you reach the turning point of your walk, blow the signal for quartering (whatever you have decided upon) and change your direction. Do this each time you turn. Your dog will eventually learn, as he follows your zigzag walk, that the whistle signal means "change direction." In time you will be able to walk straight ahead and turn your dog on signal.

If your dog still does not grasp the idea of quartering, attach a check cord about 50 feet long to his collar. Use a shorter one if he refuses to drag such a long line about. When the dog reaches the end of the line on your quartering walk, give the whistle signal for "quarter" and turn in the opposite direction, pulling the check cord as you do to make the dog turn with you. Release the pressure when he moves in the desired direction. Repeat at each turn.

For the hand signal method of teaching to quarter, your dog must have learned to retrieve. Have him sit facing you about 15 feet away. Toss the dummy with a full sweeping gesture of your right arm, giving the command to fetch as you do. (The tossing gesture should be somewhat exaggerated to clearly convey it to the dog. Start with your right hand at your left shoulder; swing your right hand and arm down, up, and then out, following through by stepping out and leaning over to your right; and end with your right arm and hand at shoulder level or slightly higher.) Have the dog make several retrieves to your right in each lesson. Continue for a week or more until he follows your instructions consistently. Then begin casting the dummy to your left, using your left hand and arm in the same exaggerated sweeping motion as described for the right-hand toss, and have him retrieve from that direction.

The dog will come to associate your arm movement and body tilt, the two components making up the hand signal, with the location of the dummy (which should be in plain sight). After a number of lessons with the left-side retrieve, mix left and right retrieves in a single lesson.

Later use two dummies, one thrown to the left and one thrown to the right. Do not send the dog out for the dummies simultaneously with the toss. After both dummies have been thrown, send the dog for the last-thrown dummy first, using the proper hand signal. When he brings in this dummy send him

Dual Ch. Towsey, is an excellent example of the Brittany's ability on the show bench and in the field. It is a credit to the breed that the same dogs can fill both roles, rather than there being one type for each.

after the first-thrown dummy, once more using the appropriate hand signal. Repeat these lessons until the dog shows he clearly understands the hand signals; this training may take about eight weeks.

To teach the hand signal for ordering the dog to go straight back, toss the dummy 15 to 20 feet behind him (as he is sitting facing you as in the previous lessons), then raise your hand over your head, make a girlish tossing motion with your hand and arm, and command "*Fetch!*"

When the dog learns these three hand signals, they can be combined with whistle signals for full direction in the field, not only for quartering but also for blind retrieves and to control pottering (not paying attention to business).

INTRODUCTION TO FEATHERS

The final phase of basic field training is introducing your dog to feathers. To do this, tie one or more pairs of pigeon, quail, or other bird wings over the dummy to completely cover it. Repeat the very first "*Fetch and Hold*" exercises that you did when you first taught him to accept a dummy. This is to accustom him to feathers in his mouth. Then practice retrieving with the feather dummy following the original training procedure with as much rapidity as the dog will allow. Later use a freshly killed but unbloodied bird with its wings tied so as not to hang and make holding difficult for the dog. Finally use a live bird with wings and legs shackled.

HARD MOUTH

If your dog shows a tendency to hard mouth—and hard mouth is not just a few tooth punctures or ruffled feathers but actually broken bones—use a wooden dummy with nails hammered in and bent across it so as to present an impenetrable object to the dog's teeth. Use this dummy for a number of training retrieves until the dog gets away from biting down hard.

4. The New Puppy

PREPARING FOR THE PUPPY'S ARRIVAL

Because at least three out of four prospective purchasers of dogs want to buy a young rather than an adult or almost adult dog, the problem of preparing for the arrival of a permanent canine house guest almost always means preparing for the arrival of a puppy. This is not to say that there is anything wrong with purchasing an adult dog; on the contrary, such a purchase has definite advantages in that it often allows freedom from housebreaking chores and rigorous feeding schedules, and these are of definite benefit to prospective purchasers who have little time to spare. Since the great majority of dog buyers, however, prefer to watch their pet grow from sprawlingly playful puppyhood to dignified maturity, buying a dog, practically speaking, means buying a puppy.

Before you get a puppy be sure that you are willing to take the responsibility of training him and caring for his physical needs. His early training is most important, as an adult dog that is a well-behaved member of the family is the end product of your early training. Remember that your new puppy knows only a life of romping with his littermates and the security of being with his mother, and that coming into your home is a new and sometimes frightening experience for him. He will adjust quickly if you are patient with him and show him what you expect of him. If there are small children in the family be sure that they do not abuse him or play roughly with him. A puppy plays hard, but he also requires frequent periods of rest. Before he comes, decide where he is to sleep and where he is to eat. If your puppy does not have a collar, find out the size he requires and buy an inexpensive one, as he will soon outgrow it. Have the proper grooming equipment on hand. Consult the person from whom you bought the puppy as to the proper food for your puppy, and learn the feeding time and amount that he eats a day. Buy him some toys—usually the breeder will give you some particular toy or toys which he has cherished as a puppy to add to his new ones and to make him less homesick. Get everything you need from your petshop *before* you bring the puppy home.

MALE OR FEMALE?

Before buying your puppy you should have made a decision as to whether you want a male or a female. Unless you want to breed your pet and raise a litter of puppies, your preference as to the sex of your puppy is strictly a personal choice. Both sexes are pretty much the same in disposition and character, and both make equally good pets.

WHERE TO BUY YOUR PUPPY

Although petshop owners are necessarily restricted from carrying all breeds in stock, they know the best dog breeders and are sometimes able to supply quality puppies on demand. In cases in which a petshop owner is unable to obtain a dog for you, he can still refer you to a good source, such as a reputable kennel. If your local petshop proprietor is unable to either obtain a dog for you or refer you to someone from whom you can purchase one, don't give up: there are other avenues to explore. The American Kennel Club will furnish you addresses. Additional sources of information are the various magazines devoted to the dog fancy.

SIGNS OF GOOD HEALTH

Picking out a healthy, attractive little fellow to join the family circle is a different matter from picking a show dog; it is also a great deal less complicated. Often the puppy will pick you. If he does, and it is mutual admiration at first sight, he is the best puppy for you. At a reliable kennel or petshop the owner will be glad to answer your questions and to point out the difference between pet and show-quality puppies. Trust your eyes and hands to tell if the puppies are sound in body and temperament. Ears and eyes should not have suspicious discharges. Legs should have strong bones; bodies should have solid muscles. Coats should be clean. Lift the hair to see if the skin is free of scales and parasites.

Temperament can vary from puppy to puppy in the same litter. There is always one puppy which will impress you by his energy and personality. He loves to show off and will fling himself all over you and his littermates, and everyone who comes to see the puppies falls in love with him. However, do not overlook the more reserved puppy. Most dogs are wary of strangers, so reserve may indicate caution, not a timid puppy. He may calmly accept your presence when he senses that all is well. Such a puppy should be a steady reliable dog when mature. In any event, never force yourself on a puppy — let him come to you. Reliable breeders and petshops will urge you to take your puppy to the veterinarian of your choice to have the puppy's health checked, and will allow you at least two days in which to have it done. It should be clearly understood whether rejection by a veterinarian for health reasons means that you have the choice of another puppy from that litter or that you get your money back.

AGE AT WHICH PUPPY SHOULD BE PURCHASED

A puppy should be at least six weeks of age before you take him home. Many breeders will not let puppies go before they are two months old. In general, the puppy you buy for show and breeding should be five or six months old. If you want a show dog, remember that not even an expert can predict with 100% accuracy what a small puppy will be when he grows up.

PAPERS

When you buy a purebred dog you should receive his American Kennel Club registration certificate (or an application form to fill out), a pedigree, and a health certificate made out by the breeder's veterinarian. The registration certificate is the official A.K.C. paper. If the puppy was named and registered by his breeder you will want to complete the transfer and send it, with the fee, to the American Kennel Club. They will transfer the dog to your ownership in their records and send a new certificate to you. If you receive, instead, an application for registration, you should fill it out, choosing a name for your dog, and mail it, with the fee, to the A.K.C.

The pedigree is a chart showing your puppy's ancestry and is not a part of his official papers. The health certificate will tell what shots have been given and when the next ones are due. Your veterinarian will be appreciative of this information, and will continue with the same series of shots if they have not been completed. The health certificate will also give the dates on which the puppy has been wormed. Ask your veterinarian whether rabies shots are required in your locality. Most breeders will give you food for a few days along with instructions for feeding so that your puppy will have the same diet he is accustomed to until you can buy a supply at your petshop.

THE PUPPY'S FIRST NIGHT WITH YOU

The puppy's first night at home is likely to be disturbing to the family. Keep in mind that suddenly being away from his mother, brothers, and sisters is a new experience for him; he may be confused and frightened. If you have a special room in which you have his bed, be sure that there is nothing there with which he can harm himself. Be sure that all lamp cords are out of his reach and that there is nothing that he can tip or pull over. Check furniture that he might get stuck under or behind and objects that he might chew. If you want him to sleep in your room he probably will be quiet all night, reassured by your presence. If left in a room by himself he will cry and howl, and you will have to steel yourself to be impervious to his whining. After a few nights alone he will adjust. The first night that he is alone it is wise to put a loud-ticking alarm clock, as well as his toys, in the room with him. The alarm clock will make a comforting noise, and he will not feel that he is alone.

YOUR PUPPY'S BED

Every dog likes to have a place that is his alone. He holds nothing more sacred than his own bed whether it be a rug, dog crate, or dog bed. If you get your puppy a bed be sure to get one which discourages chewing. Also be sure that the bed is large enough to be comfortable for him when he is fully grown. Locate it away from drafts and radiators. A word might be said here in defense of the crate, which many pet owners think is cruel and confining. Given a choice, a young dog instinctively selects a secure place

Special dog feeding and watering utensils are so designed as to safe-guard your pet from dangerous porcelain chips. These utensils are easy to keep clean, too.

in which to lounge, rest, or sleep. The walls and ceiling of a crate, even a wire one, answer that need. Once he regards his crate as a safe and reassuring place to stay, you will be able to leave him alone in the house.

FEEDING YOUR PUPPY

As a general rule, a puppy from weaning time (six weeks) to three months of age should have *four meals a day;* from three months to six months, *three meals;* from six months to one year, *two meals*. After a year, a dog does well on *one meal daily*. There are as many feeding schedules as there are breeders, and puppies do fine on all of them, so it is best for the new owner to follow the one given him by the breeder of his puppy. Remember that all dogs are individuals. The amount that will keep your dog in good health is right for him, not the "rule-book" amount. A feeding schedule to give you some idea of what the average puppy will eat is as follows:

Morning meal: Puppy meal with milk.
Afternoon meal: Meat mixed with puppy meal, plus a vitamin-mineral supplement.
Evening meal: Same as afternoon meal, but without a vitamin-mineral supplement.

Do not change the amounts in your puppy's diet too rapidly. If he gets diarrhea it may be that he is eating too much, so cut back on his food and when he is normal again increase his food more slowly.

There is a canned food made especially for puppies which you can buy only by a veterinarian's prescription. Some breeders use this very successfully from weaning to three months.

TRANSITIONAL DIET

Changing over to an adult program of feeding is not difficult. Very often the puppy will change himself; that is, he will refuse to eat some of his meals. He adjusts to his one meal (or two meals) a day without any trouble at all.

BREAKING TO COLLAR AND LEASH

Puppies are usually broken to a collar before you bring them home, but even if yours has never worn one it is a simple matter to get him used to it. Put a loose collar on him for a few hours at a time. At first he may scratch at it and try to get it off, but gradually he will take it as a matter of course. To break him to a lead, attach his leash to his collar and let him drag it around. When he becomes used to it pick it up and gently pull him in the direction you want him to go. He will think it is a game, and with a bit of patience on your part he will allow himself to be led.

DISCIPLINING YOUR PUPPY

The way to have a well-mannered adult dog is to give him firm basic training while he is a puppy. When you say *"No"* you must mean *"No."* Your dog will respect you only if you are firm. A six- to eight-weeks-old puppy is old enough to understand what *"No"* means. The first time you see your puppy doing something he shouldn't be doing, chewing something he shouldn't chew, or wandering in a forbidden area, it's time to teach him. Shout, *"No."* Puppies do not like loud noises, and your misbehaving pet will readily connect the word with something unpleasant. Usually a firm *"No"* in a disapproving tone of voice is enough to correct your dog, but occasionally you get a puppy that requires a firmer hand, especially as he grows older. In this case hold your puppy firmly and slap him gently across the hindquarters. If this seems cruel, you should realize that no dog resents being disciplined if he is caught in the act of doing something wrong, and your puppy will be intelligent enough to know what the slap was for.

After you have slapped him and you can see that he has learned his lesson, call him to you and talk to him in a pleasant tone of voice — praise him for coming to you. This sounds contradictory, but it works with a puppy. He immediately forgives you, practically tells you that it was his fault and that he deserved his punishment, and promises that it will not happen again. This form of discipline works best and may be used for all misbehaviors.

Never punish your puppy by chasing him around, making occasional swipes with a rolled-up newspaper; punish him only when you have a firm hold on him. Above all, never punish your dog after having called him to you. He must learn to associate coming to you with something pleasant.

HOUSEBREAKING

While housebreaking your puppy do not let him have the run of the house. If you do you will find that he will pick out his own bathroom, which may be in your bedroom or in the middle of the living room rug. Keep him confined to a small area where you can watch him, and you will be able to train him much more easily and speedily. A puppy does not want to dirty his bed, but he does need to be taught where he should go. Spread papers over his living quarters, then watch him carefully. When you notice him starting to whimper, sniff the floor, or run agitatedly in little circles, rush him to the place that you want to serve as his relief area and gently hold him there until he relieves himself. Then praise him lavishly. When you remove the soiled papers, leave a small damp piece so that the puppy's sense of smell will lead him back there next time. If he makes a mistake, wash the area at once with warm water, followed by a rinse with water and vinegar or sudsy ammonia. This will kill the odor and prevent discoloration. It shouldn't take more than a few days for him to get the idea of using newspapers. When he becomes fairly consistent, reduce the area of paper to a few sheets in a corner. As soon as you think he has the idea fixed in his mind, you can let him roam around the house a bit, but keep an eye on him. It might be best to keep him on leash the first few days so that you can rush him back to his paper at any signs of an approaching accident.

The normal healthy puppy will want to relieve himself when he wakes up in the morning, after each feeding, and after strenuous exercise. During early puppyhood any excitement, such as the return home of a member of the family or the approach of a visitor, may result in floor-wetting, but that phase should pass in a few weeks. Keep in mind that you can't expect too much from your puppy until he is about five months old. Before that, his muscles and digestive system just aren't under his control.

OUTDOOR HOUSEBREAKING

You can begin outdoor training on leash even while you are paper-training your puppy. First thing in the morning take him outdoors (to the curb, if you are in the city) and walk him back and forth in a small area until he relieves himself. He will probably make a puddle and then walk around, uncertain of what is expected of him. You can try standing him over a newspaper, which may give him the idea. Some dog trainers use glycerine suppositories at this point for fast action. Praise your dog every time taking him outside brings results, and he will get the idea. You'll find, when you begin the outdoor training, that the male puppy usually requires a longer walk than the female. Both male and female puppies will squat. It isn't until he is older that the male dog will begin to lift his leg. If you hate to give up your sleep, you can train your puppy to go outdoors during the day and use the paper at night.

5. Training

WHEN TO START TRAINING

You should never begin SERIOUS obedience training before your dog is seven or eight months old. (Some animal psychologists state that puppies can begin training when seven weeks old, if certain techniques are followed. These techniques, however, are still experimental and should be left to the professional trainer to prove their worth.) While your dog is still in his early puppyhood, concentrate on winning his confidence so he will love and admire you. This will make his training easier, since he will do anything to please you. Basic training can be started at the age of three or four months. He should be taught to walk nicely on a leash, sit and lie down on command, and come when he is called.

YOUR PART IN TRAINING

You must patiently demonstrate to your dog what each word of command means. Guide him with your hands and the training leash, reassuring him with your voice, through whatever routine you are teaching him. Repeat the word associated with the act. Demonstrate again and again to give the dog a chance to make the connection in his mind.

Once he begins to get the idea, use the word of command without any physical guidance. Drill him. When he makes mistakes, correct him, kindly at first, more severely as his training progresses. Try not to lose your patience or become irritated, and never slap him with your hand or the leash during the training session. Withholding praise or rebuking him will make him feel bad enough.

When he does what you want, praise him lavishly with words and with pats. Don't continually reward with dog candy or treats in training. The dog that gets into the habit of performing for a treat will seldom be fully dependable when he can't smell or see one in the offing. When he carries out a command, even though his performance is slow or sloppy, praise him and he will perform more readily the next time.

THE TRAINING VOICE

When you start training your dog, use your training voice, giving commands in a firm, clear tone. Once you give a command, persist until it is obeyed, even if you have to pull the dog to obey you. He must learn that training is different from playing, that a command once given must be obeyed no matter what distractions are present. Remember that the tone and pitch of your voice, not loudness, are the qualities that will influence your dog most.

Be consistent in the use of words during training. Confine your commands to as few words as possible and never change them. It is best for only one person to carry on the dog's training, because different people will use different words and tactics that will confuse your dog. The dog who hears *"come," "get over here," "hurry up," "here, Rex,"* and other commands when he is wanted will become totally confused.

TRAINING LESSONS

Training is hard on the dog — and on the trainer. A young dog just cannot take more than ten minutes of training at a stretch, so limit the length of your first lessons. Then you can gradually increase the length of time to about thirty minutes. You'll find that you too will tend to become impatient when you stretch out a training lesson. If you find yourself losing your temper, stop and resume the lesson at another time. Before and after each lesson have a play period, but don't play during a training session. Even the youngest dog soon learns that schooling is a serious matter; fun comes afterward.

Don't spend too much time on one phase of the training, or the dog will become bored. Always try to end a lesson on a pleasant note. Actually, in nine cases out of ten, if your dog isn't doing what you want it's because you're not getting the idea over to him properly.

YOUR TRAINING EQUIPMENT AND ITS USE

The leash is more properly called the lead, so we'll use that term here. The best leads for training are the six-foot webbed-cloth leads, usually olive-drab in color, and the six-foot leather lead. Fancier leads are available and may be used if desired.

You'll need a metal-link collar, called a choke chain, consisting of a metal chain with rings on each end. Even though the name may sound frightening, it won't hurt your dog, and it is an absolute MUST in training. There is a right and a wrong way to put the training collar on. It should go around the dog's neck so that you can attach the lead to the ring at the end of the chain which passes OVER, not under his neck. It is most important that the collar is put on properly so it will tighten when the lead is pulled and ease when you relax your grip.

The correct way to hold the lead is also very important, as the collar should have some slack in it, at all times, except when correcting. Holding the loop in your right hand, extend your arm out to the side, even with your shoulder. With your left hand, grasp the lead as close as possible to the collar, without making it tight. The remaining portion of the lead can be made into a loop which is held in the right hand. Keep this arm close to your body. Most corrections will be made with the left hand by giving the lead a jerk in the direction you want the dog to go. The dog that pulls and forges ahead can be corrected by a steady pull on the lead.

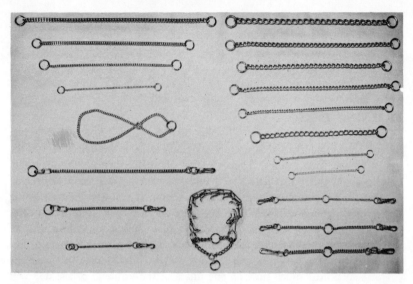

Special training collars for your dog can be purchased at your petshop.

HEELING

"*Heeling*" in dog language means having your dog walk alongside you on your left side, close to your leg, on lead or off. With patience and effort you can train your dog to walk with you even on a crowded street or in the presence of other dogs.

Now that you have learned the correct way to put on your dog's collar and how to hold the lead, you are ready to start with his first lesson in heeling. Put the dog at your left side, sitting. Using the dog's name and the command "*Heel*," start forward on your LEFT foot, giving a tug on the lead to get the dog started. Always use the dog's name first, followed by the command, such as "*Rex, heel*." Saying his name will help get his attention and will let him know that you are about to give a command.

Walk briskly, with even steps, going around in a large circle, square, or straight line. While walking, make sure that your dog stays on the left side and close to your leg. If he lags behind, give several tugs on the lead to get him up to you, then praise him for doing well. If he forges ahead or swings wide, stop and jerk the lead sharply and bring him back to the proper position. Always repeat the command when correcting, and praise him when he does well. If your dog continues to pull or lag behind, either your corrections are not severe enough or your timing between correction and praise is off. Do this exercise for only five minutes at first, gradually lengthening it to fifteen, or even half an hour.

To keep your dog's attention, talk to him as you keep him in place. You can also do a series of fast about-turns, giving the lead a jerk as you turn. He will gradually learn that he must pay attention or be jerked to your side. You can vary the routine by changing speeds, doing turns, figure-eights, and by zig-zagging across the training area.

"HEEL" MEANS "SIT," TOO

To the dog, the command *"Heel"* will also mean that he has to sit in the heel position at your left side when you stop walking — with no additional command from you. As you practice heeling, make him sit whenever you stop, at first using the word *"Sit,"* then with no command at all. He'll soon get the idea and sit down when you stop and wait for the command *"Heel"* to start walking again.

TRAINING TO SIT

Training your dog to sit should be fairly easy. Stand him on your left side, holding the lead fairly short, and command him to *"Sit."* As you give the verbal command, pull up slightly with the lead and push his hind-quarters down. Do not let him lie down or stand up. Keep him in a sitting position for a moment, then release the pressure on the lead and praise him. Constantly repeat the command as you hold him in a sitting position, thus fitting the word to the action in his mind. After a while he will begin to get the idea and will sit without your having to push his hindquarters down. When he reaches that stage, insist that he sit on command. If he is slow to obey, slap his hindquarters with your hand to get him down fast. *DO NOT HIT HIM HARD!* Teach him to sit on command facing you as well as when he is at your side. When he begins sitting on command with the lead on, try it with the lead off.

THE "LIE DOWN"

The object of this is to get the dog to lie down either on the verbal command *"Down"* or when you give him the hand signal, your hand raised in front of you, palm down. This is one of the most important parts of training. A well-trained dog will drop on command and stay down whatever the temptation: cat-chasing, car-chasing, or another dog across the street.

Don't start training to lie down until the dog is almost letter-perfect in sitting on command. Then place the dog in a sit, and kneel before him. With both hands, reach forward to his legs and take one front leg in each hand, thumbs up, and holding just below his elbows. Lift his legs slightly off the ground and pull them somewhat out in front of him. Simultaneously, give the command *"Down"* and lower his front legs to the ground.

Hold the dog down and stroke him to let him know that staying down is what you want him to do. This method is far better than forcing a young dog down. Using force can cause him to become very frightened and he will begin to dislike any training. Always talk to your dog and let him know that you are very pleased with him, and soon you will find that you have a happy working dog.

After he begins to get the idea, slide the lead under your left foot and give the command "*Down.*" At the same time, pull the lead. This will help get the dog down. Meanwhile, raise your hand in the down signal. Don't expect to accomplish all this in one session. Be patient and work with the dog. He'll cooperate if you show him just what you expect him to do.

THE "STAY"

The next step is to train your dog to stay either in a "*Sit*" or "*Down*" position. Sit him at your side. Give the command "*Stay*," but be careful not to use his name with this command, because hearing his name may lead him to think that some action is expected of him. If he begins to move, repeat "*Stay*" firmly and hold him down in the sit. Constantly repeat the word "*Stay*" to fix the meaning of that command in his mind. After he has learned to stay for a short time, gradually increase the length of his stay. The hand signal for the stay is a downward sweep of your hand toward the dog's nose, with the palm facing him. While he is sitting, walk around him and stand in front of him. Hold the lead at first; later, drop the lead on the ground in front of him and keep him sitting. If he bolts, scold him and place him back in the same position, repeating the command and all the exercise.

Use some word such as "*Okay*" or "*Up*" to let him know when he can get up, and praise him well for a good performance. As this practice continues, walk farther and farther away from him. Later, try sitting him, giving the command to stay, and then walk out of sight, first for a few seconds, then for longer periods. A well-trained dog should stay where you put him without moving until you come and release him.

Similarly, practice having him stay in the down position, first with you near him, later when you step out of sight.

THE "COME" ON COMMAND

You can train your dog to come when you call him, if you begin when he is young. At first, work with him on lead. Sit the dog, then back away the length of the lead and call him, putting into your voice as much coaxing affection as possible. Give an easy tug on the lead to get him started. When he does come, make a big fuss over him; it might help at this point to give him a small piece of dog candy or food as a reward. He should get the idea soon. You can also move away from him the full length of the lead and call to him something like "*Rex, come*," then run backward a few steps and stop, making him sit directly in front of you.

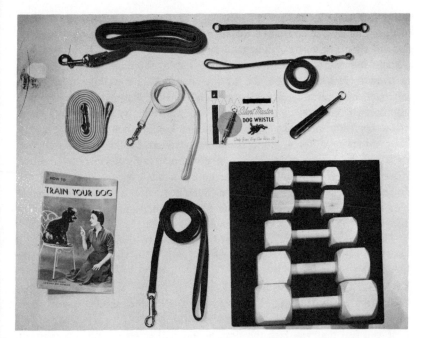

Visit your petshop for all of the training equipment you will need to make your pet a better canine citizen.

Don't be too eager to practice coming on command off lead. Wait until you are certain that you have the dog under perfect control before you try calling him when he's free. Once he gets the idea that he can disobey a command and get away with it, your training program will suffer a serious setback. Keep in mind that your dog's life may depend on his immediate response to a command to come when he is called. If he disobeys off lead, put the lead back on and correct him severely with jerks of the lead.

TEACHING TO COME TO HEEL

The object of this is for you to stand still, say "*Heel*," and have your dog come right over to you and sit by your left knee in the heel position. If your dog has been trained to sit without command every time you stop, he's ready for this step.

Sit him in front of and facing you and step back one step. Moving only your left foot, pull the dog behind you, then step forward and pull him around until he is in a heel position. You can also have the dog go around by passing the lead behind your back. Use your left heel to straighten him out if he begins to sit behind you or crookedly. This may take a little work, but he will get the idea if you show him just what you want.

THE "STAND"

Your dog should be trained to stand in one spot without moving his feet, and he should allow a stranger to run his hand over his body and legs without showing any resentment or fear. Employ the same method you used in training him to stay on the sit and down. While walking, place your left hand out, palm toward his nose, and command him to stay. His first impulse will be to sit, so be prepared to stop him by placing your hand under his body, near his hindquarters, and holding him until he gets the idea that this is different from the command to sit. Praise him for standing, then walk to the end of the lead. Correct him strongly if he starts to move. Have a stranger approach him and run his hands over the dog's back and down his legs. Keep him standing until you come back to him. Walk around him from his left side, come to the heel position, and make sure that he does not sit until you command him to.

This is a very valuable exercise. If you plan to show your dog he will have learned to stand in a show pose and will allow the judge to examine him.

TRAINING SCHOOLS AND CLASSES

There are dog-training classes in all parts of the country, some sponsored by the local humane society.

If you feel that you lack the time or the skill to train your dog yourself, there are professional dog trainers who will do it for you, but basically dog training is a matter of training YOU and your dog to work together as a team, and if you don't do it yourself you will miss a lot of fun. Don't give up after trying unsuccessfully for a short time. Try a little harder and you and your dog will be able to work things out.

ADVANCED TRAINING AND OBEDIENCE TRIALS

Once you begin training your dog and you see how well he does, you'll probably be bitten by the "obedience bug" — the desire to enter him in obedience trials held under American Kennel Club auspices.

The A.K.C. obedience trials are divided into three classes: Novice, Open, and Utility.

In the Novice Class, the dog will be judged on the following basis:

TEST	MAXIMUM SCORE
Heel on lead	35
Stand for examination	30
Heel free — off lead	45
Recall (come on command)	30
One-minute sit (handler in ring)	30
Three-minute down (handler in ring)	30
Maximum total score	200

If the dog "qualifies" in three shows by earning at least 50% of the points for each test, with a total of at least 170 for the trial, he has earned the Companion Dog degree and the letters C.D. (Companion Dog) are entered after his name in the A.K.C. records.

After the dog has qualified as a C.D., he is eligible to enter the Open Class competition, where he will be judged on this basis:

TEST	MAXIMUM SCORE
Heel free	40
Drop on Recall	30
Retrieve (wooden dumbbell) on flat	25
Retrieve over obstacle (hurdle)	35
Broad jump	20
Three-minute sit (handler out of ring)	25
Five-minute down (handler out of ring)	25
Maximum total score	200

Again he must qualify in three shows for the C.D.X. (Companion Dog Excellent) title and then is eligible for the Utility Class, where he can earn the Utility Dog (U.D.) degree in these rugged tests:

TEST	MAXIMUM SCORE
Scent discrimination (picking up article handled by master from group) Article 1	20
Scent discrimination Article 2	20
Scent discrimination Article 3	20
Seek back (picking up an article dropped by handler)	30
Signal exercise (heeling, etc., on hand signal)	35
Directed jumping (over hurdle and bar jump)	40
Group examination	35
Maximum total score	200

For more complete information about these obedience trials, write for the American Kennel Club's *Regulations and Standards for Obedience Trials*. Dogs that are disqualified from breed shows because of alteration or physical defects are eligible to compete in these trials. Besides the formal A.K.C. obedience trials, there are informal "match" shows in which dogs compete for ribbons and inexpensive trophies. These shows are run by many local fanciers' dog clubs and by all-breed obedience clubs. In many localities the humane society and other groups conduct their own obedience shows. Your local petshop or kennel can keep you informed about such shows in your vicinity, and you will find them listed in the different dog magazines or in the pet column of your local newspaper.

6. Breeding

THE QUESTION OF SPAYING

If you feel that you will never want to raise a litter of purebred puppies, and if you do not wish to risk the possibility of an undesirable mating and surplus mongrel puppies inevitably destined for execution at the local pound, you may want to have your female spayed. Spaying is generally best performed after the female has passed her first heat and before her first birthday: this allows the female to attain the normal female characteristics, while still being young enough to avoid the possible complications encountered when an older female is spayed. A spayed female will remain a healthy, lively pet. You often hear that an altered female will become very fat. However, if you cut down on her food intake, she will not gain weight.

On the other hand, if you wish to show your dog (altered females are disqualified) or enjoy the excitement and feeling of accomplishment of breeding and raising a litter of puppies, particularly in your breed and from your pet, then definitely do not spay.

Male dogs, unlike tomcats, are almost never altered (castrated).

SEXUAL PHYSIOLOGY

Females usually reach sexual maturity (indicated by the first heat cycle, or season) at eight or nine months of age, but sexual maturity may occur as early as six months or as late as thirteen months of age. The average heat cycle (estrus period) lasts for twenty or twenty-one days, and occurs approximately every six months. For about five days immediately preceding the heat period, the female generally displays restlessness and an increased appetite. The vulva, or external genitals, begin to swell. The discharge, which is bright red at the onset and gradually becomes pale pink to straw in color, increases in quantity for several days and then slowly subsides, finally ceasing altogether. The vaginal discharge is subject to much variation: in some bitches it is quite heavy, in others it may never appear, and in some it may be so slight as to go unnoticed.

About eight or nine days after the first appearance of the discharge, the female becomes very playful with other dogs, but will not allow a mating to take place. Anywhere from the tenth or eleventh day, when the discharge has virtually ended and the vulva has softened, to the seventeenth or eighteenth day, the female will accept males and be able to conceive. Many biologists apply the term "heat" only to this receptive phase rather than to the whole estrus, as is commonly done by dog fanciers.

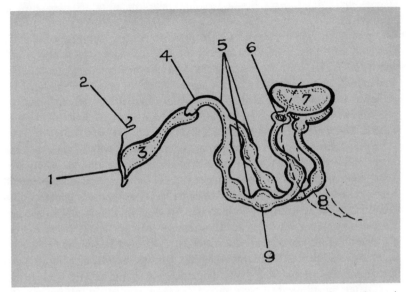

The reproduction system of the bitch: 1, vulva; 2, anus; 3, vagina; 4, cervix; 5, uterus; 6, ovary; 7, kidneys; 8, ribs; 9, fetal lump.

The ova (egg cells) from the female's ovaries are discharged into the oviduct toward the close of the acceptance phase, usually from the sixteenth to eighteenth day. From the eighteenth day until the end of the cycle, the female is still attractive to males, but she will repulse their advances. The entire estrus, however, may be quite variable: in some females vaginal bleeding ends and mating begins on the fourth day; in others, the discharge may continue throughout the entire cycle and the female will not accept males until the seventeenth day or even later.

The male dog — simply referred to by fanciers as the "dog," in contrast to the female, which is referred to as the "bitch" — upon reaching sexual maturity, usually at about six to eight months, is able, like other domesticated mammals, to breed at any time throughout the year.

The testes, the sperm-producing organs of the male, descend from the body cavity into the scrotum at birth. The condition of *cryptorchidism* refers to the retention of one or both testes within the body cavity. A testicle retained within the body cavity is in an environment too hot for it to function normally. A retained testicle may also become cancerous. If only one testicle descends, the dog is known as a *monorchid;* if neither descends, the dog is known as an *anorchid* (dog fanciers, however, refer to a dog with the latter condition as a cryptorchid). A monorchid dog is a fertile animal; an anorchid is sterile.

The male dog's penis has a bulbous enlargement at its base and, in addition, like the penis of a number of other mammals, contains a bone. When mating occurs, pressure on the penis causes a reflex action that fills the bulb with blood, swelling it to about five times its normal size within the female. This locks, or ties, the two animals together. After ejaculation, the animals usually remain tied for fifteen to thirty minutes, but they may separate very quickly or remain together an hour or more, depending on the length of time it takes for the blood to drain from the bulb.

CARE OF THE FEMALE IN ESTRUS

If you have a dog-proof run within your yard, it will be safe to leave your female in season there; if you don't have such a run, she should be shut indoors. Don't leave her alone outside even for a minute; she should be exercised only on lead. If you want to prevent the neighborhood dogs from congregating around your doorstep, as they inevitably will as soon as they discover that your female is in season, take her some distance from the house before you let her relieve herself. Take her in your car to a park or field for a chance to "stretch" her legs (always on lead of course). Keep watch for male dogs, and if one approaches take the female back to the car. After the three weeks are up you can let her out as before with no worry that she can have puppies until her next season.

Some owners find it simpler to board their female at a kennel until her season is over. However, it really is not difficult to watch your female at home. There are various products on the market which are useful at this time. Although the female in season keeps herself quite clean, sometimes she unavoidably stains furniture or rugs. You can buy sanitary belts made especially for dogs at your petshop. Consult your veterinarian for information on pills to be taken to check odor during this period. There also is a pill that prevents the female from coming in season for extended periods, and there are many different types of liquids, powders, and sprays of varying efficiency used to keep male dogs away. However, the one safe rule (whatever products you use) is: keep your bitch away from dogs that could mount her.

SHOULD YOU BREED YOUR MALE?

As with every question, whether or not to use a male dog as a stud has two sides. The arguments for and against using a dog as a stud are often very close to the ridiculous. A classic example would be the tale that once you use a dog as a stud he will lose his value as a show dog or any one of the other functions a dog may have. A sound rule may well be: *if you have a stud who has proven his worth at the shows, place his services out for hire, if only for the betterment of the breed; if your dog is not of show quality, do not use him as a stud.*

Top champion studs can bring their owners many dollars in breeding revenue. If the stud is as good as you feel he is, his services will soon be in great demand. Using a dog as a stud will not lower his value in other functions in any way. Many breeders will permit a male dog to breed an experienced female once, when about a year old, and then they begin to show their stud until he has gained his conformation championship. He is then placed out for hire through advertising in the various bulletins, journals, and show catalogs, and through the stud registers maintained by many pet-shops.

SHOULD YOU BREED YOUR FEMALE?

If you are an amateur and decide to breed your female it would be wise to talk with a breeder and find out all that breeding and caring for puppies entails. You must be prepared to assume the responsibility of caring for the mother through her pregnancy and for the puppies until they are of saleable age. Raising a litter of puppies can be a rewarding experience, but it means work as well as fun, and there is no guarantee of financial profit. As the puppies grow older and require more room and care, the amateur breeder, in desperation, often sells the puppies for much less than they are worth; sometimes he has to give them away. If the cost of keeping the puppies will drain your finances, think twice.

If you have given careful consideration to all these things and still want to breed your female, remember that there is some preparation necessary before taking this step.

WHEN TO BREED

It is usually best to breed in the second or third season. Consider when the puppies will be born and whether their birth and later care will interfere with your work or vacation plans. Gestation period is approximately fifty-eight to sixty-three days. Allow enough time to select the right stud for her. Don't be in a position of having to settle for any available male if she comes into season sooner than expected. Your female will probably be ready to breed twelve days after the first colored discharge. You can usually make arrangements to board her with the owner of the male for a few days to insure her being there at the proper time, or you can take her to be mated and bring her home the same day. If she still appears receptive she may be bred again a day or two later. Some females never show signs of willingness, so it helps to have the experience of a breeder. The second day after the discharge changes color is the proper time; she may be bred for about three days following. For an additional week or so she may have some discharge and attract other dogs by her odor, but she can seldom be bred at this time.

HOW TO SELECT A STUD

Choose a mate for your female with an eye to countering her deficiencies. If possible, both male and female should have several ancestors in common within the last two or three generations, as such combinations generally "click" best. The male should have a good show record himself or be the sire of champions. The owner of the stud usually charges a fee for the use of the dog. The fee varies. Payment of a fee does not guarantee a litter, but it does generally confer the right to breed your female again to the stud if she does not have puppies the first time. In some cases the owner of the stud will agree to take a choice puppy in place of a stud fee. You and the owner of the stud should settle all details beforehand, including such questions as what age the puppies should reach before the stud's owner can make his choice, what disposition is made of a single surviving puppy under an agreement by which the stud owner has pick of the litter, and so on. In all cases it is best that the agreement entered into by bitch owner and stud owner be in the form of a written contract.

It is customary for the female to be sent to the male; if the stud dog of your choice lives any distance you will have to make arrangements to have your female shipped to him. The quickest way is by air, and if you call your nearest airport the airline people will give you information as to the best and fastest flight. Some airlines furnish their own crates for shipping, whereas others require that you furnish your own. The owner of the stud will make the arrangements for shipping the female back to you. You have to pay all shipping charges.

PREPARATION FOR BREEDING

Before you breed your female, make sure she is in good health. She should be neither too thin nor too fat. Skin diseases must be cured before breeding; a bitch with skin diseases can pass them on to her puppies. If she has worms she should be wormed before being bred, or within three weeks afterward. It is a good idea to have your veterinarian give her a booster shot for distemper and hepatitis before the puppies are born. This will increase the immunity the puppies receive during their early, most vulnerable period. Choose a dependable veterinarian and rely on him if there is an emergency when your female whelps.

HOW OFTEN SHOULD YOU BREED YOUR FEMALE?

Do not breed your bitch after she reaches six years of age. If you wish to breed her several times while she is young, it is wise to breed her only once a year. In other words, breed her, skip a season, and then breed her again. This will allow her to gain back her full strength between whelpings.

THE IMPORTANCE AND APPLICATION OF GENETICS

Any person attempting to breed dogs should have a basic understanding of the transmission of traits, or characteristics, from the parents to the offspring and some familiarity with the more widely used genetic terms that he will probably encounter. A knowledge of the fundamental mechanics of genetics enables a breeder to better comprehend the passing, complementing, and covering of both good points and faults from generation to generation. It enables him to make a more judicial and scientific decision in selecting potential mates.

Inheritance, fundamentally, is due to the existence of microscopic units, known as *GENES,* present in the cells of all individuals. Genes somehow control the biochemical reactions that occur within the embryo or adult organism. This control results in changing or guiding the development of the organism's characteristics. A "string" of attached genes is known as a *CHROMOSOME.* With a few important exceptions, every chromosome has a partner chromosome carrying a duplicate or equivalent set of genes. Each gene, therefore, has a partner gene, known as an *ALLELE.* The number of different pairs of chromosomes present in the cells of the organism varies with the type of organism: a certain parasitic worm has only one pair, a certain fruit fly has four different pairs, man has 23 different pairs, and your dog has 39 different pairs per cell. Because each chromosome may have many hundreds of genes, a single cell of the body may contain a total of several thousand genes. Heredity is obviously a very complex matter.

In the simplest form of genetic inheritance, one particular gene and its duplicate, or allele, on the partner chromosome control a single characteristic. The presence of freckles in the human skin, for example, is believed to be due to the influence of a single pair of genes.

Each cell of the body contains the specific number of paired chromosomes characteristic of the organism. Because each type of gene is present on both chromosomes of a chromosome pair, *each type of gene is therefore present in duplicate.* The fusion of a sperm cell from the male with an egg cell from the female, as occurs in fertilization, should therefore result in offspring having a *quadruplicate number* (4) of each type of gene. Mating of these individuals would then produce progeny having an *octuplicate number* (8) of each type of gene, and so on. This, however, is normally prevented by a special process. When ordinary body cells prepare to divide to form more tissue, each pair of chromosomes duplicates itself so that there are four partner chromosomes of each kind instead of only two. When the cell divides, two of the four partners, or one pair, go into each new cell. This process, known as *MITOSIS,* insures that each new body cell contains the proper number of chromosomes. Reproductive cells (sperm cell and egg cells), however, undergo a special kind of division known as *MEIOSIS.* In meiosis, the chromosome pairs do *not* duplicate themselves, and thus when the reproductive cells reach the final dividing stage only one chromosome, or one-half of the pair, goes into each new reproductive cell. Each reproductive cell, therefore, has only half the normal number of chromosomes. These are referred to as *HAPLOID* cells, in contrast to *DIPLOID* cells, which have the full number of chromosomes.

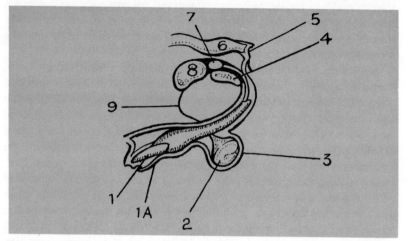

The reproductive system of a male: 1a, sheath; 1, penis; 2, testicle; 3, scrotum; 4, pelvic bone; 5, anus; 6, rectum; 7, prostate; 8, bladder; 9, vas deferens.

When the haploid sperm cell fuses with the haploid egg cell in fertilization, the resulting offspring has the normal diploid number of chromosomes.

If both partner genes, or alleles, affect the trait in an identical manner, the genes are said to be *HOMOZYGOUS*, but if one affects the character in a manner different from the other gene, or allele, the genes are said to be *HETEROZYGOUS*. For example, in the pair of genes affecting eye color in humans, if each gene of the pair produces blue eyes, the genes (and also the person carrying the genes) are said to be homozygous for blue eyes. If, however, one gene of the pair produces blue eyes, while the other gene, or allele, produces brown eyes, they are said to be heterozygous. The presence of heterozygous genes raises the question, *"Will the offspring have blue eyes or brown eyes?"* which in turn introduces another genetic principle: *DOMINANCE* and *RECESSIVENESS*.

If one gene of a pair can block the action of its partner, or allele, while still producing its own affect, that gene is said to be *dominant* over its allele. Its allele, on the other hand, is said to be recessive. In the case of heterozygous genes for eye color, the brown eye gene is dominant over the recessive blue eye gene, and the offspring therefore will have brown eyes. Much less common is the occurrence of gene pairs in which neither gene is completely dominant over the other. This, known as *INCOMPLETE* or *PARTIAL DOMINANCE*, results in a blending of the opposing influences. In cattle, if a homozygous (pure) red bull is mated with a homozygous (pure) white cow, the calf will be roan, a blending of red and white hairs in its coat, rather than either all red or all white.

During meiosis, or division of the reproductive (sperm and egg) cells, each pair of chromosomes splits, and one-half of each pair goes into one of the two new cells. Thus, in the case of eye color genes, one new reproductive cell will get the chromosome carrying the blue eye gene, while the other new reproductive cell will get the chromosome carrying the brown eye gene, and so on for each pair of chromosomes. If an organism has only two pairs of chromosomes — called pair A, made up of chromosomes A_1 and A_2, and pair B, made up of chromosomes B_1 and B_2 — each new reproductive cell will get one chromosome from each pair, and four different combinations are possible: A_1 and B_1; A_1 and B_2; A_2 and B_1, or A_2 and B_2. If the blue eye gene is on A_1, the brown eye gene on A_2, the gene for curly hair on B_1 and the gene for straight hair on B_2, each of the above combinations will exert a different genetic effect on the offspring. This different grouping of chromosomes in the new reproductive cell as a result of meiotic cell division is known as *INDEPENDENT ASSORTMENT* and is one reason why variation occurs in the offspring. In the dog, with 39 pairs of chromosomes, the possibilities of variation through independent assortment are tremendous.

But variation does not end here. For example, if two dominant genes, such as the genes for brown eyes and dark hair, were on the same chromosome, all brown-eyed people would have dark hair. Yet in instances where such joined or *LINKED* genes do occur, the two characteristics do not always appear together in the same offspring. This is due to a process known as *CROSS-OVER* or *RECOMBINATION*. Recombination is the mutual exchange of corresponding blocks of genes between the two chromosomes in a pair. That is, during cell division, the two chromosomes may exchange their tip sections or other corresponding segments. If the segments exchanged contain the eye color genes, the brown eye gene will be transferred from the chromosome carrying the dark hair gene to the chromosome carrying the light hair gene, and then brown eyes will occur with light hair, provided that the individual is homozygous for the recessive light hair gene.

Another important source of variation is *MUTATION*. In mutation, a gene becomes altered, such as by exposure to irradiation, and exerts a different effect than it did before. Most mutations are harmful to the organism, and some may result in death. Offspring carrying mutated genes and showing the effects of these mutations are known as *MUTANTS* or *SPORTS*. Mutation also means that instead of only two alleles for eye color, such as brown and blue, there may now be three or more (gray, black, etc.) creating a much larger source for possible variation in the offspring.

Further complications in the transmission and appearance of genetic traits are the phenomena known as *EPISTASIS* and *PLEIOTROPY*. Epistasis refers to a gene exerting influence on genes other than its own allele.

In all-white red-eyed (albino) guinea pigs, for example, the gene controlling intensity of color is epistatic to any other color gene and prevents that gene from producing its effect. Thus, even if a gene for red spots were present in the cells of the guinea pig, the color intensity gene would prevent the red spots from appearing in the guinea pig's white coat. *Pleiotropy* refers to the fact that a single gene may control a number of characteristics. In the fruit fly, for example, the gene that controls eye color may also affect the structure of certain body parts and even the lifespan of the insect.

One special pair of chromosomes is known as the sex chromosomes. In man, dog, and other mammals, these chromosomes are of two types, designated as X and Y. Under normal conditions, a mammal carrying two X-type sex chromosomes is a female, whereas a mammal carrying one X-type and one Y-type is a male. Females, therefore, have only X chromosomes and can only contribute X chromosomes to the offspring, but the male may contribute either an X or a Y.

If the male's sperm carrying an X chromosome fertilizes the female's egg cell (X), the offspring (XX) will be female; if a sperm carrying a Y chromosome fertilizes the egg (X), the offspring (XY) will be male. It is the male, therefore, that determines the sex of the offspring in mammals.

Traits controlled by genes present on the sex chromosome, and which appear in only one sex, are said to be *SEX LINKED*. If, for example, a rare recessive gene occurs on the X chromosome, it cannot exert its effect in the female because the dominant allele on the other X chromosome will counteract it. In the male, however, there is no second X chromosome, and if the Y chromosome cannot offer any countereffect, the recessive character will appear. There are also *SEX-LIMITED* characteristics: these appear primarily or solely in one sex, but the genes for these traits are not carried on the sex chromosomes. Sex-limited traits appear when genes on other chromosomes exert their effect in the proper hormonal (male or female) environment. Sex-linked and sex-limited transmission is how a trait may skip a generation, by being passed from grandfather to grandson through a mother in which the trait, though present, does not show.

In dealing with the simplest form of heredity — one gene effecting one character — there is an expected ratio of the offspring displaying the character to those who do not display it, depending upon the genetic makeup of the parents. If a parent is homozygous for a character, such as blue eyes, it makes no difference which half of the chromosome pair enters the new reproductive cell, because each chromosome carries the gene for blue eyes. If a parent is heterozygous, however, one reproductive cell will receive the brown eye gene while the other will receive the blue eye gene. If both parents are homozygous for blue eyes, all the offspring will receive two blue eye genes, and all will have blue eyes. If a parent is homozygous for blue eyes, and the other parent is homozygous for brown eyes, all the offspring will be heterozygous, receiving one brown eye gene and one blue eye gene, and because brown is dominant, all will have brown eyes. If both parents are heterozygous, both the blue eye gene and the brown eye gene from one parent have an equal likelihood of ending up with either the blue eye or the brown eye gene from the other parent. This results in a ratio of two heterozygous offspring to the one homozygous for brown eyes and one homozygous for blue eyes, giving a total genetic, or genotypic, ratio of $2:1:1$ or, as it is more commonly arranged, $1:2:1$. As the two heterozygous as well as the homozygous brown eye offspring will have brown eyes, the ratio of brown eyes to blue eyes (or phenotypic ratio) will be $3:1$.

If one parent is heterozygous and the other parent is homozygous for the recessive gene for blue eyes, half of the offspring will be homozygous for blue eyes and will have blue eyes, but the other half of the offspring will be heterozygous and have brown eyes. (Here both the genotypic and phenotypic ratio is $1:1$.)

If the homozygous parent, however, has the dominant gene (brown eyes), half of the offspring will be heterozygous and half will be homozygous, as before, but all will have brown eyes. By repeated determinations of these ratios in the offspring, geneticists are able to analyze the genetic makeup of the parents.

Before leaving heredity, it might be well to explain the difference between inbreeding, outcrossing, line breeding, and similar terms. Basically, there are only inbreeding and outbreeding. Inbreeding, however, according to its intensity, is usually divided into inbreeding proper and line breeding. Inbreeding proper is considered to be the mating of very closely related individuals, generally within the immediate family, but this is sometimes extended to include matings to first cousins and grandparents. Line breeding is the mating of more distantly related animals, that is, animals, not immediately related to each other but having a common ancestor, such as the same grandsire or great-grandsire. Outbreeding is divided into outcrossing, which is the mating of dogs from different families within the same breed, and cross-breeding, which is mating purebred dogs from different breeds.

From the foregoing discussion of genetics, it should be realized that the theory of telegony, which states that the sire of one litter can influence future litters sired by other studs, is simply not true; it is possible, however, if several males mate with a female during a single estrus cycle, that the various puppies in the litter may have different sires (but not two sires for any one puppy). It should also be realized that blood does not really enter into the transmission of inheritance, although people commonly speak of "bloodlines," "pure-blooded," etc.

7. Care of the Mother and Family

PRENATAL CARE OF THE FEMALE

You can expect the puppies nine weeks from the day of breeding, although 58 days is as common as 63. During this time the female should receive normal care and exercise. If she is overweight, don't increase her food at first; excess weight at whelping time is not good. If she is on the thin side, build her up, giving her a morning meal of cereal and egg yolk. Consult your veterinarian as to increasing her vitamins and mineral supplement. During the last weeks the puppies grow enormously, and the mother will have little room for food and less appetite. Divide her meals into smaller portions and feed her more ofen. If she loses her appetite, tempt her with meat, liver, chicken, etc.

As she grows heavier, eliminate violent exercise and jumping. Do not eliminate exercise entirely, as walking is beneficial to the female in whelp, and mild exercise will maintain her muscle tone in preparation for the birth. Weigh your female after breeding and keep a record of her weight each week thereafter. Groom your bitch daily — some females have a slight discharge during gestation, more prevalent during the last two weeks, so wash the vulva with warm water daily. Usually, by the end of the fifth week you can notice a broadening across her loins, and her breasts become firmer. By the end of the sixth week your veterinarian can tell you whether or not she is pregnant.

PREPARATION OF WHELPING QUARTERS

Prepare a whelping box at least a week before the puppies are to arrive and allow the mother-to-be to sleep there overnight or to spend some time in it during the day to become accustomed to it. She is then less likely to try to have her litter under the front porch or in the middle of your bed.

The box should have a wooden floor. Sides should be high enough to keep the puppies in but low enough to allow the mother to get out after she has fed them. Layers of newspapers spread over the whole area will make excellent bedding and will be absorbent enough to keep the surface warm and dry. They should be removed when wet or soiled and replaced with another thick layer. An old quilt or blanket is more comfortable for the mother and makes better footing for the nursing puppies, at least during the first week, than slippery newspaper. The quilt should be secured firmly.

SUPPLIES TO HAVE ON HAND

As soon as you have the whelping box prepared, set up the nursery by collecting the various supplies you will need when the puppies arrive. You should have the following items on hand: a box lined with towels for the puppies, a heating pad or hot water bottle to keep the puppy box warm, a pile of clean terrycloth towels or washcloths to remove membranes and to dry puppies, a stack of folded newspapers, a roll of paper towels, vaseline, rubber gloves, soap, iodine, muzzle, cotton balls, a small pair of blunt scissors to cut umbilical cords (stick them into an open bottle of alcohol so they keep freshly sterilized), a rectal thermometer, white thread, a flashlight in case the electricity goes off, a waste container, and a scale for weighing each puppy at birth.

It is necessary that the whelping room be warm and free from drafts, because puppies are delivered wet from the mother. Keep a little notebook and pencil handy so you can record the duration of the first labor and the time between the arrival of each puppy. If there is trouble in whelping, this is the information that the veterinarian will want. Keep his telephone number handy in case you have to call him in an emergency, and warn him to be prepared for an emergency, should you need him.

WHELPING

Be prepared for the actual whelping several days in advance. Usually the female will tear up papers, try to dig nests, refuse food, and generally act restless and nervous. These may be false alarms; the real test is her temperature, which will drop to below 100° about twelve hours before whelping. Take her temperature rectally at a set time each day, starting about a week before she is due to whelp. After her temperature goes down, keep her constantly with you or put her in the whelping box and stay in the room with her. She will seem anxious and look to you for reassurance. Be prepared to remove the membranes covering the puppy's head if the mother fails to do this, for the puppy could smother otherwise.

The mother should start licking the puppy as soon as it is out of the sac, thus drying and stimulating it, but if she does not perform this task you can do it with a soft rough towel, instead. The afterbirth should follow the birth of each puppy, attached to the puppy by the umbilical cord. Watch to make sure that each is expelled, for retaining this material can cause infection. The mother probably will eat the afterbirth after biting the cord. One or two will not hurt her; they stimulate milk supply as well as labor for remaining puppies. Too many, however, can make her lose her appetite for the food she needs to feed her puppies and regain her strength, so remove the rest of them along with the soiled newspapers, and keep the box dry and clean to relieve her anxiety.

If a puppy does not start breathing, wrap him in a towel, hold him upside down with his head toward the ground, and shake him vigorously. If he still does not breathe, rub his ribs briskly; if this also fails, administer artificial respiration by compressing the ribs about twenty times per minute.

If the mother does not bite the cord, or bites it too close to the body, you should take over the job to prevent an umbilical hernia. Cut the cord a short distance from the body with your blunt scissors. Put a drop of iodine on the end of the cord; it will dry up and fall off in a few days.

The puppies should follow each other at regular intervals, but deliveries can be as short as five minutes or as long as two hours apart. A puppy may be presented backwards; if the mother does not seem to be in trouble, do not interfere. But if enough of the puppy is outside the birth canal, use a rough towel and help her by pulling gently on the puppy. Pull only when she pushes. A rear-first, or breech, birth can cause a puppy to strangle on its own umbilical cord, so don't let the mother struggle too long. Breech birth is quite common.

When you think all the puppies have been whelped, have your veterinarian examine the mother to determine if all the afterbirths have been expelled. He will probably give her an injection to be certain that the uterus is clean, a shot of calcium for prevention of eclampsia, and possibly an injection of penicillin to prevent infection.

RAISING THE PUPPIES

Hold each puppy to a breast as soon as you have dried him. This will be an opportunity to have a good meal without competition. Then place him in the small box that you have prepared so he will be out of his mother's way while she is whelping. Keep a record of birth weights and take weekly readings thereafter so that you will have an accurate account of the puppies' growth. After the puppies have arrived, take the mother outside for a walk and a drink, and then leave her to take care of them. Offer her a dish of vanilla ice cream or milk with corn syrup in it. She usually will eat lying down while the puppies are nursing and will appreciate the coolness of the ice cream during warm weather or in a hot room. She will not want to stay away from her puppies more than a minute or two the first few weeks. Be sure to keep water available at all times, and feed her milk or broth frequently, as she needs liquids to produce milk. To encourage her to eat, offer her the foods she likes best, until she "asks" to be fed without your tempting her. She will soon develop a ravenous appetite and should be fed whenever she is hungry.

Be sure that all the puppies are getting enough to eat. Cut their claws with special dog "nail" clippers, as they grow rapidly and scratch the mother as the puppies nurse. Normally the puppies should be completely weaned by six weeks, although you may start to give them supplementary feedings at three weeks. They will find it easier to lap semi-solid food.

As the puppies grow up, the mother will go into the box only to nurse them, first sitting up and then standing. To dry up her milk supply completely, keep her away from her puppies for longer periods. After a few days of part-time nursing she will be able to stay away for much longer periods of time, and then completely. The little milk left will be resorbed.

When the puppies are five weeks old, consult your veterinarian about temporary shots to protect them against distemper and hepatitis; it is quite possible for dangerous infectious germs to reach them even though you keep their living quarters sanitary. You can expect the puppies to need at least one worming before they are ready to go to their new homes, so take a stool sample to your veterinarian before they are three weeks old. If one puppy has worms, all should be wormed. Follow your veterinarian's advice.

The puppies may be put outside, unless it is too cold, as soon as their eyes are open (about ten days), and they will benefit from the sunlight. A rubber mat or newspapers underneath their box will protect them from cold or dampness.

HOW TO TAKE CARE OF A LARGE LITTER

The size of a litter varies greatly. If your bitch has a large litter she may have trouble feeding all of the puppies. You can help her by preparing an extra puppy box. Leave half the litter with the mother and the other half in a warm place, changing their places at two-hour intervals at first. Later you may change them less frequently, leaving them all together except during the day. Try supplementary feeding, too, as soon as their eyes are open.

CAESAREAN SECTION

If your female goes into hard labor and is not able to give birth within two hours, you will know that there is something wrong. Call your veterinarian for advice. Some females must have Caesarean sections (taking puppies from the mother by surgery), but don't be alarmed if your dog has to undergo this. The operation is relatively safe. She can be taken to the veterinarian, operated on, and then be back in her whelping box at home within three hours, with all puppies nursing normally a short time later.

8. Health

WATCHING YOUR PUPPY'S HEALTH

First, don't be frightened by the number of diseases a dog can contract. The majority of dogs never get any of them. Don't become a dog-hypochondriac. All dogs have days when they feel lazy and want to lie around doing nothing. For the few diseases that you might be concerned about, remember that your veterinarian is your dog's best friend. When you first get your puppy, select a veterinarian who you feel is qualified to treat dogs. He will get to know your dog and will be glad to have you consult him for advice. A dog needs little medical care, but that little is essential to his good health and well-being. He needs:

1. Proper diet at regular hours
2. Clean, roomy housing
3. Daily exercise
4. Companionship and love
5. Frequent grooming
6. Regular check-ups by your veterinarian

THE USEFUL THERMOMETER

Almost every serious ailment shows itself by an increase in the dog's body temperature. If your dog acts lifeless, looks dull-eyed, and gives the impression of illness, check his temperature by using a rectal thermometer. Hold the dog and insert the thermometer, which should be lubricated with vaseline, and take a reading. The average normal temperature is 101.5° F. Excitement may raise this value slightly, but any rise of more than a few points is a cause for alarm. Consult your veterinarian.

FIRST AID

In general, a dog will heal his wounds by licking them. If he swallows anything harmful, chances are that he will throw it up. But it will probably make you feel better to help him if he is hurt, so treat his wounds as you would your own. Wash out the dirt and apply an antiseptic. If you are afraid that your dog has swallowed poison and you can't get to the veterinarian fast enough, try to induce vomiting by giving him a strong solution of salt water or mustard and water. Amateur diagnosis is dangerous, because the symptoms of so many dog diseases are alike. Too many people wait too long to take their dog to the doctor.

IMPORTANCE OF INOCULATIONS

With the proper series of inoculations, your dog will be almost completely protected against disease. However, it occasionally happens that the shot does not take, and sometimes a different form of the virus appears against which your dog may not be protected.

DISTEMPER

Probably the most virulent of all dog diseases is distemper. Young dogs are most susceptible to it, although it may affect dogs of all ages. The dog will lose his appetite, seem depressed, chilled, and run a fever. Often he will have a watery discharge from his eyes and nose. Unless treated promptly, the disease goes into advanced stages with infections of the lungs, intestines, and nervous system, and dogs that recover may be left with some impairment such as paralysis, convulsions, a twitch, or some other defect, usually spastic in nature. The best protection against this is very early inoculation with a series of permanent shots and a booster shot each year thereafter.

HEPATITIS

Veterinarians report an increase in the spread of this viral disease in recent years, usually with younger dogs as the victims. The initial symptoms — drowsiness, vomiting, great thirst, loss of appetite, and a high temperature — closely resemble those of distemper. These symptoms are often accompanied by swellings of the head, neck, and abdomen. The disease strikes quickly; death may occur in just a few hours. Protection is afforded by injection with a vaccine recently developed.

LEPTOSPIROSIS

This disease is caused by bacteria that live in stagnant or slow-moving water. It is carried by rats and dogs; infection is begun by the dog's licking substances contaminated by the urine or feces of infected animals. The symptoms are diarrhea and a yellowish-brown discoloration of the jaws, tongue, and teeth, caused by an inflammation of the kidneys. This disease can be cured if caught in time, but it is best to ward it off with a vaccine which your veterinarian can administer along with the distemper shots.

RABIES

This is an acute disease of the dog's central nervous system. It is spread by infectious saliva transmitted by the bite of an infected animal. Rabies is generally manifested in one of two classes of symptoms. The first is "furious rabies," in which the dog shows a period of melancholy or depression, then irritation, and finally paralysis. The first period lasts from a few hours to several days. During this time the dog is cross and will change his position often. He loses his appetite for food and begins to lick, bite, and swallow foreign objects. During the irritative phase the dog is spasmodically wild and has impulses to run away. He acts in a fearless manner and runs and bites at everything in sight. If he is caged or confined he will fight at the bars, often breaking teeth or fracturing his jaw. His bark becomes a peculiar howl. In the final, or paralytic, stage, the animal's lower jaw becomes paralyzed and hangs down; he walks with a stagger and saliva drips from his mouth. Within four to eight days after the onset of paralysis, the dog dies.

The second class of symptoms is referred to as "dumb rabies" and is characterized by the dog's walking in a bearlike manner, head down. The lower jaw is paralyzed and the dog is unable to bite. Outwardly it may seem as though he had a bone caught in his throat.

Even if your pet should be bitten by a rabid dog or other animal, he probably can be saved if you get him to the veterinarian in time for a series of injections. However, after the symptoms have appeared no cure is possible. But remember that an annual rabies inoculation is almost certain protection against rabies. If you suspect your dog of rabies, notify your local Health Department. A rabid dog is a danger to all who come near him.

COUGHS, COLDS, BRONCHITIS, PNEUMONIA

Respiratory diseases may affect the dog because he is forced to live under man-made conditions rather than in his natural environment. Being subjected to cold or a draft after a bath, sleeping near an air conditioner or in the path of a fan or near a radiator can cause respiratory ailments. The symptoms are similar to those in humans. The germs of these diseases, however, are different and do not affect both dogs and humans, so they cannot be infected by each other. Treatment is much the same as for a child with the same type of illness. Keep the dog warm, quiet, and well fed. Your veterinarian has antibiotics and other remedies to help the dog recover.

INTERNAL PARASITES

There are four common internal parasites that may infect your dog. These are roundworms, hookworms, whipworms, and tapeworms. The first three can be diagnosed by laboratory examination; the presence of tapeworms is determined by seeing segments in the stool or attached to the hair around the tail. Do not under any circumstances attempt to worm your dog without the advice of your veterinarian. After first determining what type of worm or worms are present, he will advise you of the best method of treatment.

EXTERNAL PARASITES

The dog that is groomed regularly and provided with clean sleeping quarters should not be troubled by fleas, ticks, or lice. If the dog should become infested with any of these parasites, he should be treated with a medicated dip bath or the new oral medications that are presently available.

SKIN AILMENTS

Any persistent scratching may indicate an irritation. Whenever you groom your dog, look for the reddish spots that may indicate eczema, mange, or fungal infection. Rather than treating your dog yourself, take him to the

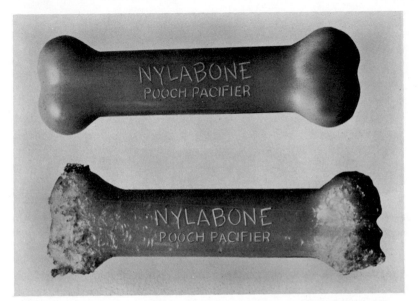

Nylabone, the new chew-toy for dogs that won't chip or break. The top photo shows a new Nylabone, below is one that has been chewed and pounded by a hammer without splintering or breaking.

veterinarian, as some of the conditions may be difficult to eradicate and can cause permanent damage to his coat.

EYES, EARS, TEETH, AND CLAWS

If you notice foreign matter collecting in the corners of your dog's eyes, wipe it out with a piece of cotton or tissue. If there is a discharge, check with your veterinarian.

Examine your dog's ears daily. Remove all visible wax, using a piece of cotton dipped in a boric acid solution or a solution of equal parts of water and hydrogen peroxide. Be gentle and don't probe into the ear, but just clean the parts you can see.

Don't give your dog bones to chew: they can choke him or puncture his intestines. Today veterinarians and dog experts recommend Nylabone, a synthetic bone manufactured by a secret process, that can't splinter or break even when pounded by a hammer. Nylabone will keep puppies from chewing furniture, aid in relieving the aching gums of a teething pup, and act as a toothbrush for the older dog, preventing the accumulation of tartar. Check your dog's mouth regularly and, as he gets older, have your veterinarian clean his teeth twice a year.

To clip your dog's claws, use specially designed clippers that are available at your petshop. Never take off too much of the claw, as you might

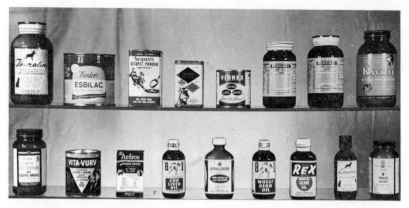

Active dogs and breeding bitches need food supplements. Visit your petshop for fresh vitamins and minerals to be added to your dog's diet.

cut the quick, which is sensitive and will bleed. Be particularly careful when you cut claws in which the quick is not visible. If you have any doubts about being able to cut your dog's claws, have your veterinarian or petshop do it periodically.

CARE OF THE AGED DOG

With the increased knowledge and care available, there is no reason why your dog should not live to a good old age. As the years go by he may need a little additional care. Remember that an excessively fat dog is not healthy, particularly as he grows older, so limit the older dog's food accordingly. He needs exercise as much as ever, although his heart cannot bear the strain of sudden and violent exertion. Failing eyesight or hearing means lessened awareness of dangers, so you must protect him more than ever.

Should you decide at this time to get a puppy, to avoid being without a dog when your old friend is no longer with you, be very careful how you introduce the puppy. He naturally will be playful and will expect the older dog to respond to his advances. Sometimes the old dog will get a new lease on life from a new puppy, but he may be consumed with jealousy. Do not give the newcomer the attention that formerly was exclusively the older dog's. Feed them apart, and show your old friend that you still love him the most; the puppy, not being accustomed to individual attention, will not mind sharing your love.

9. Showing

There is no greater pleasure for the owner than showing a beautiful dog perfectly groomed and trained for the show ring. Whether he wins or not, it is gratifying to show a dog in superb condition, one that is a credit to your training and care. A great deal of preparation, both for you and your dog, is needed before the day that you do any serious winning. Showing is not so easy as it looks, even if you have a magnificent dog. He must be presented to the judge so that all of his good points are shown to advantage. This requires practice in gaiting, daily grooming from puppyhood, and the proper diet to make him sound in body.

When you buy your puppy you probably will think he is the best in the country and possibly in the world, but before you enter the highly competitive world of dog shows, get some unbiased expert opinion. As your dog matures, compare him with the standard of his breed. Visit a few dog shows as a spectator and make mental notes of what is required of the handlers and dogs. Watch how the experienced handlers manage their dogs to bring out their best points.

TYPES OF DOG SHOWS

There are various types of dog shows. The American Kennel Club sanctioned matches are shows at which purebred dogs may compete, but not for championship points. These are excellent for you to enter to accustom you and your dog to showing. If your dog places in a few match shows, then you might seriously consider entering the big-time shows. An American Kennel Club all-breed show is one at which purebred dogs compete for championship points. An American Kennel Club specialty show is for one breed only. It may be held in conjunction with an all-breed show (by designating the classes at that show as its specialty show) or it may be held entirely apart. Obedience trials are different in that in them the dog is judged according to his obedience and ability to perform, not by his conformation to the breed standard.

There are two types of championship conformation shows: *benched* and *unbenched*. At a benched show your dog must be on his appointed bench during the advertised hours of the show's duration. He may be removed from the bench only to be taken to the exercise pen or to be groomed (an hour before showing) in an area designated for handlers to set up their crates and grooming tables. At an unbenched show your car may serve as a bench for your dog.

To become a champion your dog must win fifteen points in competition with other dogs; a portion of the fifteen points must be awarded as major point wins (three to five points) under different judges.

HOW TO ENTER

If your dog is purebred and registered with the AKC — or eligible for registration — you may enter him in the appropriate show class for which his age, sex, and previous show record qualify him. You will find coming shows listed in the different dog magazines or at your petshop. Write to the secretary of the show, asking for the premium list. When you receive the entry form, fill it in carefully and send it back with the required entry fee. Then, before the show, you should receive your exhibitor's pass, which will admit you and your dog to the show. Here are the five official show classes:

PUPPY CLASS: Open to dogs at least six months and not more than twelve months of age. Limited to dogs whelped in the United States and Canada.

NOVICE CLASS: Open to dogs six months of age or older that have never won a first prize in any class other than the puppy class, and less than three first prizes in the novice class itself. Limited to dogs whelped in the United States or Canada.

BRED BY EXHIBITOR CLASS: Open to all dogs, except champions, six months of age or over which are exhibited by the same person, or his immediate family, or kennel that was the recognized breeder on the records of the American Kennel Club.

AMERICAN-BRED CLASS: Open to dogs that are not champions, six months of age or over, whelped in the United States after a mating which took place in the United States.

OPEN CLASS: Open to dogs six months of age or over, with no exceptions.

In addition there are local classes, the Specials Only class, and brace and team entries.

For full information on dog shows, read the book *HOW TO SHOW YOUR OWN DOG,* by Virginia Tuck Nichols. (T.F.H.)

ADVANCED PREPARATION

Before you go to a show your dog should be trained to gait at a trot beside you, with head up and in a straight line. In the ring you will have to gait your dog around the edge with other dogs and then individually up and down the center runner. In addition the dog must stand for examination by the judge, who will look at him closely and feel his head and body structure. He should be taught to stand squarely, hind feet slightly back, head up on the alert. Showing requires practice training sessions in advance. Get a friend to act as judge and set the dog up and "show" him a few minutes every day.

Sometime before the show, give your dog a bath so he will look his best. Get together all the things you will need to take to the show. You will want to take a water dish and a bottle of water for your dog (so he won't be affected by a change in drinking water). Take your show lead, bench chain (if it is a benched show), combs and brush, and the identification ticket sent by the show superintendent, noting the time you must be there and the place where the show will be held, as well as the time of judging.

THE DAY OF THE SHOW

Don't feed your dog the morning of the show, or give him at most a light meal. He will be more comfortable in the car on the way, and will show more enthusiastically. When you arrive at the show grounds, find out where he is to be benched and settle him there. Your bench or stall number is on your identification ticket, and the breed name will be on placards fastened to the ends of the row of benches. Once you have your dog securely fastened to his stall by a bench chain (use a bench crate instead of a chain if you prefer), locate the ring where your dog will be judged (the number and time of showing will be on the program of judging which came with your ticket). After this you may want to take your dog to the exercise ring to relieve himself, and give him a small drink of water. Your dog will have been groomed before the show, but give him a final brushing just before going into the show ring. When your breed judging is called, it is your responsibility to be at the ringside ready to go in. The steward will give you an armband which has on it the number of your dog.

Then, as you step into the ring, try to keep your knees from knocking! Concentrate on your dog and before you realize it you'll be out again, perhaps back with the winners of each class for more judging and finally, with luck, it will be over and you'll have a ribbon and trophy.

ENCYCLOPEDIA OF DOG BREEDS, by Ernest H. Hart. ·This is the most complete all-breed dog book ever written. Every recognized breed as well as many that are virtually unknown in America is illustrated and discussed. The book contains six large color sections and a wealth of black and white photos and line drawings. History, management and care of all dogs is included along with new and fascinating breed information. This

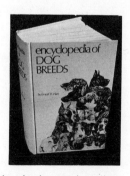

classic in canine literature is available at your pet shop or book store. Published by T.F.H. Publications.

BIBLIOGRAPHY

Breed Your Dog, Dr. Leon Whitney, 64 pp., $1.00. Illustrated throughout with instructive photographs in both color and black and white. Covers aspects of breeding through puppyhood.

Dollars In Dogs, Leon F. Whitney, D.V.M., 255 pp., $6 95. Twenty-six chapters on different vocations in the vast field of dog business. An excellent book for your library.

First Aid For Your Dog, Dr. Herbert Richards, 64 pp., $1.00. Illustrated throughout in both color and black and white.

Groom Your Dog, Leon F. Whitney, D.V.M., 64 pp., $1.00. Illustrated throughout with both color and black and white photographs showing various grooming techniques.

How To Feed Your Dog, Dr. Leon F. Whitney, 64 pp., $1.00. Best diets and feeding routines for puppies and adult canines. Profusely illustrated in color and black and white.

How To Housebreak And Train Your Dog, Arthur Liebers, 80 pp., $1.00. Six educational chapters on training your dog. Illustrated in color and black and white photographs.

How To Raise And Train A Pedigreed Or Mixed Breed Puppy, Arthur Liebers, 64 pp., $1.00. Nine chapters covering such canine questions as choosing your puppy through breeding the adult. Illustrated in both color and black and white photographs.

How To Show Your Dog, Virginia Tuck Nichols, 252 pp., $6.95. This book is written for the novice who plans to show his dog. An excellent text to make your dog library complete.

The Distemper Complex, Leon F. Whitney, D.V.M., and George D. Whitney, D.V.M., 219 pp., $6.95. A comprehensive canine health book. Nineteen revealing chapters. A thirty-nine-page bibliography. Completely indexed.

This Is The Puppy, Ernest Hart, 190 pp., $6.95. Eleven profusely-illustrated chapters to guide the reader in the care and selection of a puppy. Full-color photographs. Also black and white candids. Indexed.